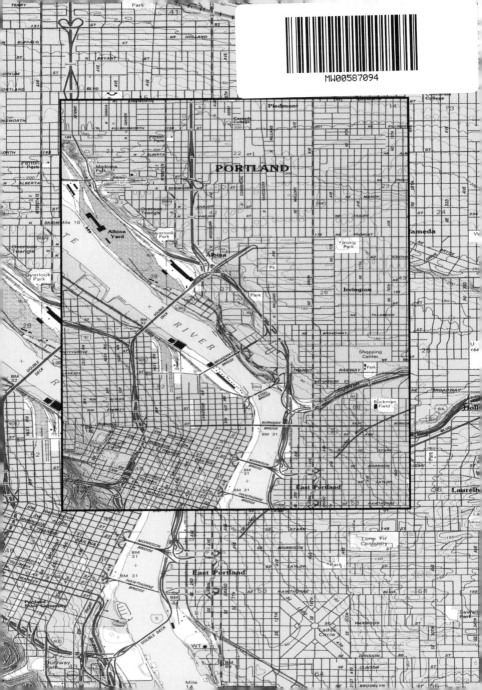

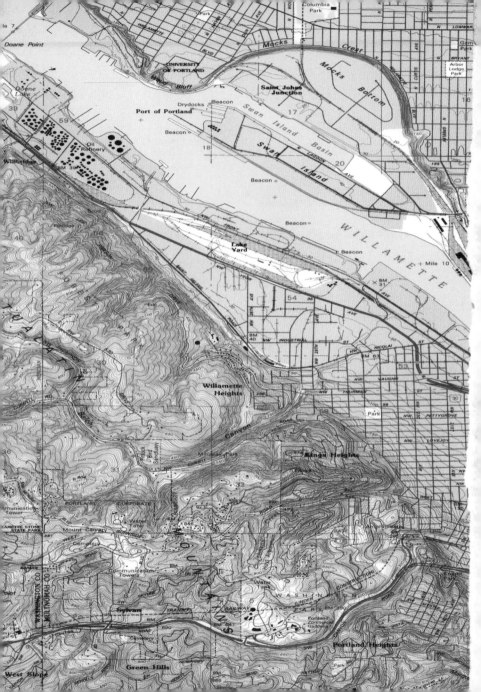

PORTLAND
COCKTAILS

AN ELEGANT COLLECTION
OF OVER 100 RECIPES
INSPIRED BY THE CITY OF ROSES

NICOLE SCHAEFER

CIDER MILL
PRESS

BOOK
PUBLISHERS

PORTLAND COCKTAILS

ISBN-13: 978-1-64643-355-1
ISBN-10: 1-64643-355-6

This book may be ordered by mail from the publisher. Please include $5.99 for postage and handling. Please support your local bookseller first!

Books published by Cider Mill Press Book Publishers are available at special discounts for bulk purchases in the United States by corporations, institutions, and other organizations. For more information, please contact the publisher.

Cider Mill Press Book Publishers
"Where good books are ready for press"
501 Nelson Place
Nashville, Tennessee 37214
cidermillpress.com

Typography: London Oatmeal, Avenir, Copperplate, Sackers, Warnock

Back cover image by Aubrie LeGault (see page 165).
Photography Credits on page 263

Printed in China

1 2 3 4 5 6 7 8 9 0
First Edition

CONTENTS

INTRODUCTION

How to describe Portland? Portland is . . . well, weird. The residents prefer it that way. If anything, Portland embraces it's uniqueness and lives up to the depiction of it in the popular television show *Portlandia*. It's a city of polar opposites. On one hand, there are the hippies with their Birkenstocks and marijuana and buying (and selling) handmade goods at Saturday Market. On the other hand, there are the yuppies who populate the Pearl District and the West Hills. Indeed, you can cross a bridge and end up in a completely different environment than where you just were. Portland is also "the Silicon Forest" due to tech companies such as Intel that are headquartered here. Portland is the home of Nike, too. Rabid legions of fans support the Trailblazers (the basketball team), the Timbers (the soccer team), as well as the rival college football teams, the Ducks and the Beavers.

Portland is known for many different things—from the bridges that cross the Willamette River to its proximity to both the ocean and the mountains, where the residents enjoy a multitude of outdoor sports. If you have never been to Portland, you'll likely be confused by the way the city is laid out. There is a NW and a NE and a SW and a SE—separated by Burnside Street as well as the Willamette (Will-a-met) River. Each area has a distinct personality and there is almost a sense of being in a different city from area to area. NW is a mix of trendy and tech—home to not only NW 23rd Avenue and the Pearl District, but also most of the Intel employees and young families. SW

is characterized by the West Hills—full of large, beautiful old homes, as well as downtown Portland, the cultural center of the city. NE is a mix of distinguished areas such as Irvington and more urban-feeling neighborhoods, such as Hollywood. SE is fun and funky and also houses Reed College, which has a gorgeous campus.

Essentially, Portland has it all. Not only that, but we also have the Rose Garden and the Japanese Garden and a Chinese Garden. Portland has also become a mecca of sorts for foodies and people who love craft beer, craft cider, and craft cocktails.

Much like the food culture, the cocktail scene is dominated by

top-level mixologists creating artful cocktails from only the finest ingredients, from top-notch distilleries, like Aviation Gin and Westward Whiskey. Not only will you find some excellent bars here, you'll also find fun and unique ones, like Hale Pele—a tiki-themed bar in NE Portland (see page 90). Much like the city's neighbor-hoods, there's a cocktail bar to fit everyyone's tastes: Raven's Manor is an incredibly immersive experience for anyone who enjoys the dark and spooky (see page 116); the Sports Bra is the first sports bar devoted to women's sports, and Sucker Punch is a bar that only serves nonalcoholic cocktails.

A BRIEF HISTORY OF COCKTAILS IN PORTLAND

Although Portland is now on the map for the many bars and their accompanying craft cocktails, it appears cocktail culture didn't really appear in Portland until the 1990s. Portland has more of a history with alcohol than with cocktails.

In the mid-nineteenth century, Portland was apparently populated mostly by young unmarried men. As one might suspect, this meant the activities engaged by this population were less than wholesome. In 1855, Portland boasted one drinking establishment for every 50 citizens. By the 1860s, Portland had attracted the attention of German immigrants and most of the bars began to sell Henry Weinhard beer.

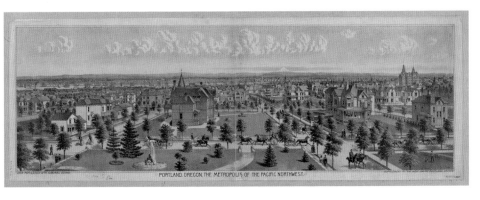
PORTLAND, OREGON. THE METROPOLIS OF THE PACIFIC NORTHWEST.

In 1897, a man named Jonathan Bourne, a Boss Tweed-like figure, rented out 19 rooms in Salem's Eldridge Block to keep Oregon's representatives politically aligned with him drunk and happy for 40 days. In Bourne's words, "I hired the best chef in the state of Oregon, sent him to Salem to fix up apartments in the Eldridge Block; things to eat and drink and entertainment. I said to the chef: 'I pay all expenses. I want to take care of all my friends in the lower House who signed pledges with me, the friends of Silver." This assisted in establishing Oregon's national reputation as a moral sinkhole filled with booze.

With this reputation came a call to ban booze altogether. After some fighting amongst those who were pro-booze and those who were anti-booze, women won the battle to ban alcoholic libations in Oregon, with the ban going into effect in 1914, years before national Prohibition.

Portland's Prohibition began on January 2, 1916. This simply led to Portland becoming a haven for bootleggers. George Baker, the mayor of Portland in 1917, took over the speakeasy scene. Portland apparently had a reputation as the "driest city in America." But this was

simply a facade. According to the memoirs of Floyd Marsh, a former Portland police officer and Prohibition expert, there were probably around 100 speakeasies, 40 gambling dens, and a monthly bribe total of $100,000.

In 1933, Prohibition ended nationally, and Oregon created the Oregon Liquor Control Commission, which to this day oversees all liquor activity in the state. It wasn't until more than 70 years later that Portland's cocktail scene really exploded again, when bars like Teardrop Lounge opened and put the city's bar scene on the national map.

References to Portland's seedy past exist in several bars. Examples include the Multnomah Whiskey Library, which feels like a secret hidden in a non descript building downtown. Another bar that feels hidden is the Scotch Lodge, located in the depths of a building that looks like a school. There are also bars that feel like they are whisking you away to a special location, such as Bible Club. No matter where you wander in Portland, however, you are bound to end up somewhere with great cocktails.

HOW TO STOCK YOUR HOME BAR
LIKE A PORTLANDER

Portland bartending and mixology are all about simple and fresh. This explains the city's motto about cocktails: "It's the maker, not the equipment." However, if one wants to enter the world of cocktails, some equipment is necessary.

GLASSWARE

Collins glass

Coupe

Spanish coffee mug

Rocks glass

Tiki mug

Moscow Mule mug

TOOLS

Bar spoon

Basic measuring tool (like a
    jigger)

Mixing glass

Muddler

Punch bowl

Shaker

Strainer

SPIRITS

Aviation Gin

Prosecco

Hayman's Old Tom Gin

Aperol

Cynar

Rye Whiskey

Rhum Agricole

Velvet Falernum

Pama

Dry Curaçao

Aquavit

Wray + Nephew White
    Overproof Rum

Coruba Dark Rum

Hamilton 151

Hamilton Pot-Still Gold

Plantation 3-Star

Herbsainte

Carribbean Black-Spiced Rum

Lillet Blanc

Aria Dry Gin

St. Germain Elderflower Liqueur

Blended Scotch

Cherry Heering

12 Bridges Gin

Kahlúa

Triple Sec

Sweet Vermouth

Benedictine

Absinthe

Lovejoy Vodka

Buffalo Trace Bourbon

Calvados

Green Chartreuse

Creme de Violette

Blue Curaçao

Cointreau

Arbbeg Single Malt Scotch Whiskey

Fino Sherry

Japanese Whiskey

Cognac

Amontillado Sherry

Hendricks Gin

Cachaca

Bourbon

Rum (Light, Medium, Dark)

Vodka

Reposado Tequila

BITTERS, SYRUPS, TONIC, AND OTHER INGREDIENTS

Angostura Bitters

Ginger Beer

Perfect Puree Concentrates

Peychaud's

Tonic Water

Soda Water

Limes

Lemons

Oranges

Mint

HOW TO DRINK LIKE A PORTLANDER

It's "Organ" not "Or-e-gun." Also don't say "couch" like the living room furniture. It's pronounced "Cooch."

Yes, we know that Burnside is where Mr. Burns from *The Simpsons* got his name. There's also a Flanders Street.

You should probably sip your craft beer and cocktails from a hand-made glass you bought at Saturday market, while rocking a scarf and a hemp hat.

Whenever possible, use fresh, local ingredients and make your own syrups and purees and bitters. You can even make your own infused vodka.

Beer is never a bad idea. Especially if it is accompanied by trivia. Pub trivia.

Always drink while watching the Trail Blazers or Timbers. And preferably go to a sports bar.

Play a boardgame or an old-school video game while drinking. This can be achieved either at home or at one of our arcades, like Quarterworld.

Dogs should be anywhere and everywhere at all times.

If possible, run a race before drinking. In the rain.

Go to a festival and make a friend or two. Always look for the Unipiper too, and if you're lucky, you might see the Mermaid Parade. Then give some tickets away because they gave you too many!

A PORTLAND BUCKET LIST

The Naked Bike Ride: If that's your thing. It's literally a bike ride with hundreds or thousands of naked people riding bikes. Don't bring the kids though. Or you'll have some 'splaining to do!

Escape Rooms: Portland has a ton of escape rooms. They're incredibly fun.

Shakespeare in the Park: The Portland Actors Ensemble does Shakespeare in area parks. It makes for a very funneth time! (BYOB.)

Race Around the Portland International Raceway: Basically it is what it sounds like, but much, much louder than you think.

Pittock Mansion: Explore this gorgeous historical landmark. Just ignore the creepy mannequins.

Rent a Bicycle: There's no better way to explore the city than on bike, and, hey, you'll blend in with the locals!

Explore All of the Districts: Well, maybe not all of them, as there are almost 100 districts, but definitely Alberta, Pearl, Hawthorne, and Mississippi.

The Shanghai Tunnels: Part of Portland's not-so-pleasant past, the Shanghai Tunnels are a fascinating journey back in time. And it's said that they are haunted.

Our Lady's Grotto: This sanctuary includes a peace garden, a meditation chapel, a rose garden, and shrines. No matter what you worship, this is a nice break from the city proper.

Go on a Submarine: Visit the Oregon Museum of Science and Industry (OMSI) and tour an actual submarine! And OMSI After Dark is one of the best ways to explore the museum (no children allowed).

Powell's: Seriously, what are you waiting for? It's a full city block of books.

Movie at a Brewpub: Yeah we're sort of big on that here. And it's pretty awesome. Go check out McMenamin's Bagdad Theater and see a movie while chowing down and drinking ale.

Oregon Historical Museum: Filled with over 85,000 artifacts and documents, this museum even has the famous penny with which the name "Portland" was chosen.

Portland Center Stage: There's always something worth checking out from the largest theater company in the city.

Pioneer Square: Don't be a square; be sure to hit this urban gathering spot that's great for people-watching—it's called "Portland's living room" for a reason, after all.

The Gorge: Not technically Portland, but we'll let it slide. The Gorge is beautiful and not to be missed. (Hiking is optional.)

Multnomah Falls: Again, not technically Portland, but they are in the Gorge and they are Gorge-us (sorry, couldn't resist).

Forest Park: Yup, we have a witchy castle. In a park. Forest Park. It has nothing to do with witches, it just looks neat.

Stark's Vacuum Museum: Suck it up, we all learn new things every day. Like that there's a vacuum museum here.

Float Down a River: This is a very popular activity amongst residents and visitors alike when the days get warmer.

Oregon Holocaust Memorial: It's always important to pay respect to the past.

Glowing Greens: Play mini golf. In the dark. With pirates! Need I say more?

Weird Selfies: Under the Keep Portland Weird Sign south of the Burnside Bridge or across the street from Voodoo Donuts.

Take an Axe to Paul Bunyan: But don't, actually. Just go visit his statue in the Kenton neighborhood.

Ride the Tram: Not just any tram, but the Aerial Tram, which gives you incredible views.

Revolution Hall: This place is the coolest. It's a former high school and now they have concerts and cocktails.

See the Goats: No, not the greatest of all time. Actual goats. That live in Belmont. Who might be the greatest goats of all time. But that's subjective.

Cherry Blossoms: If you are here at the right time of the year, you can see the 100 Akebono cherry trees that line Waterfront Park. Yes, it's amazing.

The Queen: Darcelle XV is royalty—the oldest working drag queen.

The World's Smallest Park: Visit so you can say you did. It's at the intersection of two streets in Southwest Portland, and it's called Mill Ends Park.

Street Art: Yes, the Portland Art Museum is wonderful, but don't miss all of the public art; maps are available online.

Roller Derby: Go see the Rose City Rollers do their thing, and be glad you're not one of them.

International Rose Test Garden: Stop and smell the roses. Even if you hate flowers and bugs, this is a neat garden. From someone who hates flowers and bugs.

Lan Su Chinese Garden: It's been called "the most authentic Chinese garden outside of China." It's absolutely breathtaking and you won't remember you are in Old Town, which is a good thing.

Freakybuttrue Pecularium: There are no catchy phrases for this one. It's a place with a bunch of strange stuff, like a sundae filled with bugs. It's truly odd. And free.

Saturday Market: When you shop at one of the biggest open-air markets in the country, you're bound to find cool stuff. You might even see Elvis.

Stumptown Coffee: You can't come to Portland and not have coffee. That might actually be illegal. Anyway, if you're in need of an afternoon boost, Stumptown is one of the best places to grab one.

Drink Beer: Nothing more to say about that.

IF YOU HAVE ONLY 24 HOURS IN PORTLAND:

Stop at Voodoo Donuts.

Go to Saturday Market for some homemade crafts.

Shop at Powell's Books.

Explore Hawthorne Boulevard.

Walk the waterfront and take in the sights.

Eat lunch in the Japanese Garden.

Catch some improv at Comedy Sportz.

Check out a movie at the Hollywood Theater.

And, obviously, visit as many bars as possible.

FOOD

Voodoo Donuts: You Do so well—of course Voodoo donuts must be mentioned. It's a unique experience with even more unique donuts.

Lardo: Those dirty, dirty fries—covered with pork scraps, fried herbs, parmesan cheese, and marinated peppers.

Pine State Biscuits: Wash those fries down with some biscuits.

Food Trucks: Still hungry? Check out the food trucks! They're all over Portland, including one devoted to potatoes.

Bollywood Theater: Amazing Indian street food.

Salt & Straw: You're probably stuffed, but there's always room for ice cream, amirite? If so, get thee to a Salt & Straw!

IF YOU HAVE 10 MEALS IN PORTLAND:

MASALA LAB PDX
5237 NE Martin Luther King Jr Blvd, Portland, OR 97211.
This brand-new Indian-American brunch spot is all that and a side of naan!

TARTUCA
3951 N Mississippi Ave, Portland, OR 97227.
An intimate Italian spot with delicious food.

KANN
548 SE Ash St, Portland, OR 97214
A long-anticipated Haitian restaurant is finally open.

OX
2225 NE MLK Jr Blvd
Home to heavenly chops, chorizo, and rib eyes. Argentine Barbeque at its finest.

AKADI
1001 SE Division St.
Portland's only sit-down West African Restaurant.

APIZZA SCHOLLS
4741 SE Hawthorne Blvd.
Some of the best pizza you will ever have. But get there right when it opens so you can snag a table.

HIGGINS
1239 SW Broadway
The last restaurant with a chef from the first round of Portland's James Beard Award-winning chefs in the 1990s, Higgins has excellent burgers and lots of local gems.

AFURI IZAKAYA
Multiple locations
A delicious ramen restaurant beloved by locals.

ANDINA
Absolutely delicious Andean food.

SHALOM Y'ALL
Fabulous Mediterranean food.

PORTLAND PERSONALITIES

AVOCADO-DAIQUIRI

HEAVEN

MANDARIN KISS

ANDALUSIAN BUCK

CLYDE COMMONS' TEQUILA

SHERRY EGGNOG

FORMOSA FIZZ COCKTAIL

AMARETTO SOUR

PILSNER VS. APEROL

PEPPER SMASH #2

CORELEONE

Upon doing research for this book, it became clear that no work featuring the cocktails of Portland would be complete without interviewing the people most synonymous with Portland cocktails. The first person interviewed was Jeffrey Morganthaler and upon his insistence, the second was Lucy Brennan. Both of these well-known bartenders proved to be down-to-earth, extremely nice, and full of great advice and information about cocktails. Their reputations are clearly earned and it is certain that they will continue to shape the cocktail scene in Portland for years to come.

LUCY BRENNAN

Lucy Brennan seems to be synonymous with cocktail culture in Portland. In fact, Jeffrey Morganthaler (see page 42) insists that she essentially created cocktail culture in Portland. Brennan has worked at various area bars and restaurants and even has her own book of cocktail recipes.

How did you become interested in cocktails in the first place?
LB: I think because I was fortunate enough to start working at Saucebox downtown. So I opened that bar with Bruce Carey, who used to be the owner. I started off as a bartender and then after a couple of months I became the bar manager and really got free rein to be creative and to come up with some really fun cocktails. This was the mid-1990s. That's how I got into it, and that's how I was able to be creative, and not have the requirements of making basic cocktails. Not that there's anything wrong with that.

How do you think Portland's cocktail scene has evolved over the years?

LB: Well, since I've been bartending in Portland, since 1995, I think Portland was one of the first cities in the nation to start the cocktail revolution. I shouldn't say started, but be part of it. It was really fun to watch every restaurant have their own craft cocktail menu available, which was new, so that was really fun. I think it went through a period of being a bit over-ambitious. I've never been a fan of the term "mixologist." I'm a bartender. At that time, I had my own restaurant and just kind of kept my head down. I would go to Tales of the Cocktails in New Orleans. And that was really fun because that's when it was getting its own momentum—dissecting the bartending. Before that, people just bartended to get through college. It's different now, people look at it differently.

What do you think was the beginning of cocktails in Portland?

LB: Before Saucebox opened, in 1995, a couple of places that aren't around anymore were doing fantastic cocktails. One place was Brazen Bean, that was in NW Portland, and then it was Zephyro, and I worked at Zephyro because Bruce also owned that. And that was definitely, you know, again, bridging the kitchen and the bar. Making simple syrups, making different kinds of purees, and tapping into the whole farmers market scene. That evolved the bar too, that program. So as far as when did it start, I would have to say early 1990s.

What do you think makes Portland's bar scene unique compared to other cities?

LB: Well, I don't know if that's the case anymore, because I feel like everyone has really come up to speed. I feel like the farmers market is in every city, and like every little district within the city, and that has a huge impact. I think the public has really wanted to become educated when it comes to spirits. You've got all the small distilleries and the microbreweries. So it really unfolded naturally. I don't know where we're at now considering the last two years of the pandemic. It's nice to see people go back out and enjoy really well-thought-out drinks that aren't ambitious.

Any favorite stories from your time behind the bar?
LB: *Laughs* Well, what kind of stories? You mean, drink-wise?

What's the worst order you've ever gotten?
LB: Oh my gosh, no, you can't ask me that. I think it was in the 1990s, someone ordered a single malt scotch with Diet Coke. I was like, hell no, I'm not going to put those together. But I guess the funniest story for me behind the bar is when I came up with this drink called the Avocado Daiquiri. Basically, it was guacamole in a glass. It was disgusting. My friends thought I was nuts. It took years to perfect. It became one of those ugly ducklings that becomes a swan. As far as customers having impressions on me, um, they're all wonderful.

What's your favorite cocktail to make personally?
It depends. In the winter, I really enjoy black Manhattans. In the summer, you know, a really good Last Word or Gimlet. Really simple and clean. And you think they would be easy to make, but it's one of those things. It's kind of like if you go in and order someone's Daiquiri. It's a telltale sign if a bartender can make those drinks really, really well. I really like Spritz Hugo. It's not an Aperol Spritz but you drink it at the same time. You know, the happy hour, the aperitif hour in Italy.

What is essential for novice cocktail makers to have in their home bars? Do you think there's any essential equipment or essential ingredients?
LB: Definitely bitters. Definitely a good mixing glass. Good ice. As far as equipment, those are the items I want to have. As far as the prod-

ucts to have at home in order to make basic drinks? A really well-made bourbon, an elegant gin, a handsome vodka, a fun tequila. What else? Those would be the four I start with.

When I was in Las Vegas recently, I saw an automated cocktail bar where people could order drinks and a machine would make them. Do you think machines will eventually replace bartenders?

LB: Bartenders are always going to be around. It's one of the oldest crafts. Especially now, coming out of Covid, when people want that interaction. They work in Vegas, they may have that demand, but definitely a no. A hard no.

What's your process for creating cocktails? How do you start usually?

LB: It depends on what I'm doing and what spirit I'm using. I always blind-taste myself on the spirit. What I mean by that is that I smell it. I get the notes—similar to wine-tasting. See what I get from it. And then see how I can build on it without overpowering it. For me, you really want to showcase the spirit. You want to elevate. Some people put too many ingredients in, and for me, I want to keep it below five. Five is the maximum probably. Four ingredients to a cocktail I think is really smart.

Is there one absolute no-no in cocktail making?

LB: Oh, no, not off the top of my head. Nope. When I said about the bartending scene becoming too ambitious, that's what I meant. Too many ingredients.

And what do you think makes a drink more culinary? How can people elevate their cocktails at home without over-complicating them?

LB: If you go to the farmers market, and you have something you really like, like apricots or what's in season right now. Take those and you can make your own infusions. You can make an apricot martini or something really simple. Not something over the top with like eighteen ingredients in it, where you're like, "Oh, there's tequila in that." Your drink should be well balanced. Flavorful, approachable, and well balanced.

Lucy Brennan's Cocktails taken from her book *Hip Sips*.

· AVOCADO DAIQUIRI ·

Brennan has two methods of creating the signature lemon-lime juice blend seen in most of her cocktails. The recipe included here is the less labor-intensive version. Brennan recommends pairing this drink with a burger or spicy ceviche.

GLASSWARE: Balloon wineglass

GARNISH: Pomegranate concentrate

- 2 oz. silver rum
- 2 oz. gold rum
- ¼ medium-ripe avocado, peeled and pitted
- ½ oz. half-and-half
- ¼ oz. Lemon-Lime Juice
- 2 oz. simple syrup
- 1 ½ cups cocktail ice cubes

1. In a blender, combine all of the ingredients with the ice and blend for 20 to 30 seconds, or until the mixture is silky smooth with no trace of ice; the consistency of the drink should be similar to heavy cream.

2. Pour the cocktail into the balloon wineglass and lightly zigzag the pomegranate concentrate over the top. Place a small drink straw or toothpick at the top of the zigzag pattern and pull through the center to make a series of pomegranate hearts.

LEMON-LIME JUICE: In a glass container, combine 1 (16 oz.) bottle Santa Cruz 100% Lime Juice and 1 (16 oz.) bottle Santa Cruz 100% Lemon Juice and shake vigorously to mix. Store in the refrigerator for up to 7 days.

· HEAVEN ·

Brennan is a world traveler and created this cocktail which blends the orange and sweet vanilla of Tuaca, the nutty, creamy taste of Saint Brendan's, and the coffee notes of Tia Maria.

GLASSWARE: Heat-resistant wineglass (8 oz.)

- ½ oz. Tuaca Brandy
- 1 oz. Tia Maria Liqueur
- 1 oz. Saint Brendan's Irish Cream liqueur

- 3 oz. strong hot coffee
- 2 heaping tablespoons Vanilla Whipped Cream

1. Combine the 3 liqueurs in the wineglass and top with the coffee, leaving an inch of space at the top of the glass.

2. Add the whipped cream and serve with a straw, holding the hot glass by the stem.

VANILLA WHIPPED CREAM: In a chilled stainless-steel bowl, beat 1 cup heavy whipping cream with an electric mixer on high speed. As the cream begins to thicken, gradually add ¼ oz. Monin Vanilla Syrup and beat until soft peaks form.

· MANDARIN KISS ·

B rennan describes this cocktail as a "toast to odd couples" and recommends pairing it with a lamb burger.

GLASSWARE: Bucket glass
GARNISH: Orange slice

- 2 oz. Maker's Mark Bourbon
- 2 tablespoons Mandarin Puree
- Splash of soda water
- 1 orange slice for garnish

1. Fill a tempered glass with cocktail ice cubes and add the bourbon and puree. Cap the glass with a stainless-steel cocktail shaker and shake vigorously for 10 seconds.

2. Pour the drink and ice into the bucket glass, leaving about 1 inch of space at the top of the glass.

3. Top off the drink with soda water and garnish with the orange slice.

MANDARIN PUREE: Peel, segment, and if necessary, seed 4 mandarin oranges. In a blender, combine the fruit with 1 tablespoon sugar and 1 teaspoon fresh lemon juice and pulse until completely chopped. Puree until smooth. Taste the puree and add more sugar or lemon juice as desired. Use immediately, or freeze for up to 6 months. Makes 1 cup.

JEFFREY MORGANTHALER

In Portland, the name "Jeffrey Morganthaler" is inextricably linked with cocktails. He has a way of creating unique, yet familiar cocktails and did so for years while working at Clyde Commons. Morganthaler is now on to other adventures, but still had time to answer some questions.

How did you become interested in cocktails? How did you get started?
How did I get started? Well, I went to architecture school at the University of Oregon in the 1990s, and I needed a summer job, back in 1996. I went to the career center and there weren't a ton of paying architecture jobs because they usually offer internships for no pay, which was not going to work for me. But I saw a bartending job, and I'd never tended bar before. I'd never even spent much time in bars, but I thought it sounded like a cool job and I applied and got my first bartending job.

Besides you, who would you say has influenced the Portland cocktail scene? And who influenced you?

Oh, I mean hands down, the most important person in Portland bartending is Lucy Brennan (see page 32). She really brought cocktails to Oregon, and to Portland, was really the first person to put Portland on a larger stage for doing something different and unique. She released a book, I want to say in the early 2000s, called *Hip Sips*, full of recipes from her establishments, the two establishments that she had, and it was super influential.

How do you think Portland's cocktail scene has evolved since you started?

When I got here, there was just a small handful of bartenders kind of doing interesting cocktails. Portland hadn't really hit the main stage yet. And during my time here, I was able to watch things blow up. As more people moved here, the city was placed on a national and international stage for culture, and for dining, and for drinking, and wine and beer and stuff, and so nowadays it's hard to get a bad drink because there are so many fantastic bars in Portland.

What's your favorite bar?

I have two, probably. Hey Love (see page XXX), which is a hotel bar just around the corner from the bar that I'm opening, which is also in a hotel. Really amazing, super progressive drinks program, progressive hospitality, a really incredible bar. And then, I really love Palomar (see page XXX), which is my friend Ricky Gomez's bar. He's a Cuban guy and it's a Cuban bar, and just so you know, something very different in Portland, a very tropical bar, not the kind of bar you'd traditionally find in Portland.

What do you think makes Portland's bar scene unique?

Oregon in general has sort of been defined by a kind of DIY mentality and that has really been reflected in the cocktail-bar world, especially in the past 15 years or so. People creating, really taking matters into their own hands and creating their own ingredients and creating their own styles and recipes.

What's your favorite cocktail to make, for yourself?

Probably an Old-Fashioned. It's one of the drinks we're most known for at our bar.

What do you think is essential for novice bartenders to have in their home bars?

I always recommend a good shaker and a good strainer. I'm not one to go for super fancy expensive equipment. I think that it's the craftsman and not the tools. But I think a shaker and a strainer and some sort of way to measure things are indispensable.

I saw an automated cocktail bar in Las Vegas. Do you think bartenders will be rendered obsolete at some point?

Nope. I don't. *Laughs.* I think that those automated bar things are probably going to end up being used in Vegas instead of bartenders working behind the scenes making drinks for tables, but they'll never be able to replace the experience of going in and sitting at a bar and talking to a bartender. That's just not how it works.

What's your process for creating cocktails?

My process . . . I mean, it's similar to any design process. I start with a concept and kind of flesh that out as fully as I can, and then I just begin working to try and execute that concept. And there's a fair amount of trial and error in the execution, but once I have a really solid concept, it usually comes together very quickly.

Do you think that your architecture training assisted with that at all?
Yeah, I would say so.

Is there one absolute no-no in cocktail making—like nobody should ever do *blank*?
No, not really. I think that being too prescriptive in this kind of stuff is a bad thing. Drink whatever you like.

What makes a drink more culinary, in your opinion? How can a home bartender elevate their cocktails and make them more culinary?
Culinary really comes down to the preparation of cocktails. And you don't have to take a culinary tack to create a great drink. Culinary comes in the preparation of homemade ingredients and syrups, and that kind of stuff. But if you just want to make a really good Martini or Negroni, there's no need for culinary skills.

· ANDALUSIAN BUCK ·

Morganthaler concocted this cocktail around 2010 while working for Clyde Commons. It's wonderful because it's not too much of anything—not too sweet, not too sour, and not too boozy. All of the ingredients balance perfectly to create a one-of-a-kind experience. Morganthaler recommends making homemade ginger beer, but store-bought works in a pinch.

GLASSWARE: Collins glass

GARNISH: Lime wheel

- 1 oz. gin
- 1 oz. Amontillado sherry
- ½ oz. fresh lime juice
- 1 teaspoon rich demerara syrup (2:1)
- 2 oz. Homemade Ginger Beer

1. Combine all of the ingredients in a cocktail shaker with ice and shake until cold.

2. Add the ginger beer directly to the shaker and then strain slowly into the chilled collins glass over ice.

3. Garnish with the lime wheel.

HOMEMADE GINGER BEER:

(base recipe makes 1 (16-oz.) bottle of ginger beer, so multiply the proportions by the number of bottles you plan to use): In a bowl, combine 1 oz. ginger juice, 2 oz. finely strained fresh lemon juice, 2 oz. simple syrup, and 11 oz. warm water (cold water if using a soda siphon). Mix the ingredients together. If using a soda siphon, pour all of the ingredients into the canister, screw on the lid, charge with CO_2, shake once, and refrigerate. If using a bottle, fill each bottle with 16 oz. of the mixture and add about 25 granules of champagne yeast. Seal the cap securely, shake well, and store for 48 hours—no more and no less—in a warm and dark place. After 48 hours, refrigerate immediately to halt the process.

· CLYDE COMMONS' ·
TEQUILA-SHERRY EGGNOG

This drink made its debut at Clyde Commons in 2009—fun and quirky, it still retains the classic taste of a traditional eggnog. This recipe makes two servings.

GLASSWARE: Chilled cups

GARNISH: Dusting of freshly grated nutmeg

- 2 large eggs
- 3 oz. superfine or baker's sugar
- 2 oz. Añejo tequila
- 2½ oz. Amontillado sherry
- 6 oz. whole milk
- 4 oz. heavy cream

1. In a stand mixer on low speed, beat the eggs until smooth. Slowly add the sugar until incorporated and dissolved. Slowly add the remaining ingredients.

2. Refrigerate overnight and dust with fresh nutmeg before serving.

· FORMOSA FIZZ · COCKTAIL

This cocktail clearly draws inspiration from the Clover Club. However, Jeffrey has put his own twist on this classic by using tequila instead of gin.

GLASSWARE: **Champagne glass**

GARNISH: **Fresh raspberries**

- 1½ oz. blanco tequila
- ¾ oz. fresh lemon juice
- ½ oz. raspberry syrup
- ½ oz. fresh egg white
- ¼ oz. rich simple syrup
- 1½ oz. chilled soda water

1. Combine all of the ingredients, except the soda water, in a cocktail shaker filled with ice, shake until chilled and foamy, and strain into the Champagne glass.

2. Top with the soda and garnish with fresh raspberries.

· AMARETTO SOUR ·

Morganthaler swears he makes the best Amaretto Sour in the world. His secret? Using cask-proof bourbon and an immersion blender prior to shaking to ensure that the egg whites get extra fluffy.

GLASSWARE: Chilled rocks glass
GARNISH: Lemon peel and brandied cherry

- 1½ oz. Amaretto
- ¾ oz. cask-proof bourbon
- 1 oz. fresh lemon juice
- 1 teaspoon rich simple syrup (2:1)

- ½ oz. fresh egg white
- Garnishes: lemon peel and brandied cherry

1. Shake the ingredients without ice for about 10 to 15 seconds. Add ice to the shaker and shake again until chilled.

2. Strain into the chilled rocks glass over ice and garnish with the lemon and the cherry.

RYAN MAGARIAN

Ryan Magarian is a local legend in Portland hospitality with an international reputation. He is the co founder of Aviation American Gin and Oven and Shaker Pizzeria and Bar in the Pearl District, for which he created the cocktail menu. Magarian has also been involved with the development and team-trainings of over 100 restaurants, bars, and brands worldwide.

This is a Ryan Magarian original, and it is delicious.

GLASSWARE: Highball glass

GARNISH: Hop buds

- 1 oz. Aperol
- 1 oz. freshly pressed grapefruit juice
- ½ teaspoon clover honey syrup (combine and completely integrate two parts syrup to one part warm water)

- 2 oz. Bitburger Premium Pilsner
- 3 oz. club soda
- 1 dash Bittern's Hopped Grapefruit Bitters

1. Combine all of the ingredients in the highball glass and stir well.

2. Fill the glass with ice and garnish with a sprinkling of fresh hop buds.

How could I pass up including a cocktail with bell pepper juice?

- 12–15 mint leaves
- 2 oz. Krogstad Aquavit
- ¾ oz. fresh lime juice
- ¾ oz. fresh yellow bell pepper juice
- ¾ oz. blended Grade A maple syrup (2:1 syrup to water)

1. Add the ingredients in order, starting with the mint, and then press the combination together at least three times with a muddler.

2. Fill the shaker with ice, shake vigorously for 8 seconds, and then double-strain into the chilled old-fashioned glass over ice.

3. Garnish with the double mint sprig.

· CORELEONE ·

This one includes Aviation Gin, of which Magarian is a cofounder (see page 242 for more on Aviation Gin).

GLASSWARE: Chilled cocktail glass
GARNISH: A green grape

- 5 green grapes
- 1 ½ oz. Aviation American Gin
- ½ oz. Clear Creek Distillery Grappa di Sangiovese
- ½ oz. freshly pressed lemon juice
- ½ oz. simple syrup
- 2 dashes Regan's No. 6 Orange Bitters

1. Add the grapes to a cocktail shaker and muddle the grapes.

2. Combine the remaining ingredients in the shaker with ice, shake vigorously for 8 seconds, and double-fine strain into the chilled cocktail glass.

3. Garnish with the single green grape, sliced at its tip and rested on the rim of the glass.

NW PORTLAND

GLITTER

MOJITO DE PIÑA

SACSAYHUAMAN

MELONES CON AJI

GOODNIGHT, MOON

THE FLOATING WORLD

FLEUR-DE-LIS

TETON TANYA

L‍et's talk NW. Portland that is. NW Portland is hip and trendy, well, parts of it. If hip and trendy is what you are seeking, you'll need to go to "Trendy-third" as locals call it—also known as NW 23rd. There you'll find a plethora of fun restaurants and shops. If you're seeking more of a sophisticated experience, you'll want to check out the Pearl District and the even newer Slabtown District. If residential/suburban life is what you are seeking to explore, drive over Burnside and you'll enter the quieter, more family-oriented side of NW Portland. Of course, you can still find cocktails out in suburbia (it is Portland, after all).

Speaking of trendy, this restaurant is definitely on brand, serving Mediterranean food with a side of craft cocktails.

· GLITTER ·

The name of this cocktail seems pretty self explanatory—the bubbles from the Prosecco make it seem like you are drinking a glass full of glitter.

GLASSWARE: Cocktail glass

- Ginger Sugar
- Prosecco or dry sparkling wine

- 1 oz. Ginger Syrup

1. Rim a cocktail class with the Ginger Sugar.

2. Fill the rimmed glass to ½ inch shy of the top with chilled Prosecco or sparkling wine.

3. Finish with 1 oz. Ginger Syrup.

GINGER SUGAR: In a food processor, pulse together 6 cut-up large pieces of candied ginger with ¼ cup granulated sugar; do not overmix as doing so will cause the sugar to heat up and clump. You want to achieve an even, fine-grain texture. Store in an airtight container.

GINGER SYRUP: In a small saucepan over medium heat, combine 1 cup sugar and 1 cup water, stir, and heat until the sugar is fully dissolved. Use a box grater to mince fresh ginger root until you have about ¼ cup of juice and ginger pulp. Combine the pulp and the simple syrup and refrigerate for 30 minutes to an hour then pour through a sieve to remove the pulp.

ANDINA

1314 NW GLISAN ST.

Andina is a must if you are in Portland. This Peruvian restaurant is all
that and a bag of yucca fritters. Delicious and fresh, even their cocktails
are memorable, such as the one below.

· MOJITO DE PIÑA ·

What is clearly Andina's take on a classic Mojito, the Mojito de Piña takes it up a notch with fresh pineapple and pineapple-infused rum.

GLASSWARE: Rocks glass

- 1 ½ oz. pineapple-infused gold rum
- 1 oz. fresh lime juice
- 1 oz. pineapple puree
- 5 basil leaves, torn in half
- 1 ½ tablespoons bar sugar
- 1 oz. ice water

1. Combine all of the ingredients in a cocktail shaker with ice, shake well, and pour into the rocks glass.

This one's spicy! Keep a glass of water close by.

GLASSWARE: Cocktail glass
GARNISH: Cilantro leaf

- 1 ½ oz. Pepper Vodka
- 2 oz. Passion Fruit Simple Syrup Mix (made from six parts passion fruit puree and 4 parts simple syrup)

1. Combine the vodka and simple syrup mix in a cocktail shaker with ice, shake well, and strain into a cocktail glass.

2. Garnish with the cilantro leaf.

PEPPER VODKA: Place 6 habanero peppers in a jar, fill with Monopolowa Vodka, and store in a cool, dry place for about a week. Strain and use.

• MELONES CON AJI •

This Greg Hoitsma cocktail is Andina in a glass. Fresh cantaloupe puree mixed with lime and cucumber—can you get any more refreshing than that?

GLASSWARE: Cocktail glass

GARNISH: Lime zest, and a mixture of paprika and cayenne pepper

- 1½ oz. Hendrick's Gin
- 2 oz. fresh cantaloupe puree
- 1 oz. fresh lime juice
- 1½ tablespoons baker's sugar
- 1 oz. cucumber water

1. Combine the gin, cantaloupe, lime juice, and sugar in a cocktail shaker with ice, shake well, and strain into the cocktail glass.

2. Float the cucumber water on top and dust with lime zest and a mix of paprika and cayenne pepper.

TEARDROP LOUNGE

1015 NW EVERETT ST.

Teardrop Lounge has been taking charge of the cocktail renaissance in Portland since 2007. It is located right in the heart of Portland's Pearl District. You can't miss it!

· GOODNIGHT, MOON ·

I t's hard to describe this incredibly extraordinary cocktail, which combines fennel-walnut soda with heavy cream and the appley taste of Pommeau de Normandie.

GLASSWARE: Collins glass

- 1 oz. Pommeau de Normandie
- ½ oz. heavy cream
- 2 ½ oz. Fennel-Walnut Soda
- 1 oz. club soda

1. Build the drink in the collins glass over ice and stir to combine.

FENNEL-WALNUT SODA: Combine equal parts maple-walnut syrup and fresh fennel juice and stir well.

· THE FLOATING WORLD ·

This drink will make you feel like you are floating on a cloud.

GLASSWARE: Coupe

GARNISH: Edible flower

- 1½ oz. Hayman's Old Tom Gin
- ½ oz. Lustau Rose Vermut
- ½ oz. cranberry juice
- 3 dashes garlic bitters
- 8 drops saline tincture
- 1 oz. Kimino Ume Plum Soda

1. Combine all of the ingredients, except the soda, in a mixing glass with ice, stir, and strain into the coupe.

2. Top with the soda and garnish with the edible flower.

· FLEUR-DE-LIS ·

This drink certainly evokes France with its combination of cognac and wine.

GLASSWARE: Rocks glass

- 1 oz. Peychaud's Bitters
- ¾ oz. Pierre Ferrand Ambre Cognac
- ¾ oz. Montinore Verjus
- ¼ oz. honey water (2:1)
- 2 lemon peels
- Brut sparkling wine

1. Combine all of the ingredients, except the sparkling wine, in a mixing glass with ice, stir, and strain into the rocks glass over a single large ice cube.

2. Top with the sparkling wine.

G-LOVE NEW AMERICAN KITCHEN

1615 NW 21ST AVE.

Portland's first reverse steakhouse, G-Love is relatively new to the Portland scene. What's a reverse steakhouse? It's a restaurant where vegetables are the main attraction and the proteins are side dishes. How very Portland!

· TETON TANYA ·

Inspired by the classic Boulevardier cocktail, this Collin Nicholas cocktail combines dry, spice-driven Cynar with bright, bittersweet Aperol.

GLASSWARE: Rocks glass
GARNISH: Spritz of Becherovka and an orange peel

- 1 oz. Aperol
- 1 oz. Cynar
- 1 oz. Rye whiskey

1. Combine all of the ingredients in a mixing glass with ice, stir, and strain into the rocks glass over a single large ice cube.

2. Garnish with a spritz of Becherovka and an orange peel.

NE PORTLAND

DEPARTMENT OF AGRICOLE COCKTAIL
MANHATTAN AND A 1/2
POMEGRANATE COSMO
AMERICAN TROUBADOUR
THE PRINCE OF EDINIA
SCANDINAVIAN DAIQUIRI
SECRET OF THE LOST LAGOON
TAKIN' A BREAK ROSÉ COCKTAIL
SUGAR REPORT
SLEEPING LOTUS
A'A'PO'E
POLE STAR
TICO TICO
SIGNAL FIRE
HURRICANE DROPS
THE DUKE
CHILI CHILLY BANG BANG
OX BLOOD COCKTAIL

NE Portland is a mix of detached-single-family-home neighborhoods and denser blocks of apartment buildings. One thing is for sure though, NE has tons of bars, and with those, tons of craft cocktails. You can even grab one to go while you walk along Broadway or around Burnside.

BLANK SLATE

7201 NE GLISAN ST., SUITE C

Blank Slate is a bar in the Montavilla
neighborhood. And in fact, Blank Slate
calls themselves a neighborhood bar—
serving upscale food and drinks in an
inviting atmosphere. Blank Slate is also a
woman-owned business.

• DEPARTMENT OF AGRICOLE COCKTAIL •

Created by Blank Slate owner Kierre Van de Veere, this cocktail takes a tropical drink base and adds some bitter notes with burnt sugar simple syrup. Blank Slate uses Rhum J. M.

GLASSWARE: Coupe

GARNISH: Lemon twist

- 1 ½ oz. unaged rhum agricole
- 1 oz. fresh lime juice
- ½ oz. John D. Taylor's Velvet Falernum
- ¼ oz. cold-brew coffee
- ¼ oz. coffee liqueur
- ¼ oz. Burnt Sugar Simple Syrup

1. Combine all of the ingredients in a cocktail shaker with ice, shake well, and double-strain into the coupe.

2. Garnish with the lime wheel.

BURNT SUGAR SIMPLE SYRUP: Boil 1 cup white sugar and ½ cup water over medium-high heat, stirring constantly, until the mixture becomes caramel brown. Remove the pan from heat, add ½ cup warm water carefully, because it will steam and bubble, and stir until combined. Let it cool before use. Store in the refrigerator for up to 2 weeks.

WONDERLY
4727 NE FREMONT ST.

Wonderly is well . . . a wonder. It looks
vintage inside with stools lining a round bar.
And the drinks are a wonder too.

Creator Kate Wood describes this drink as "an extra-delicious take on the classic," and it is definitely extra delicious.

GLASSWARE: Chilled Nick and Nora glass
GARNISH: Cocktail cherries on a pick

- **3 oz. Bottled-in-bond bourbon**
- **1 oz. House Sweet Vermouth Blend (1:1 Carpano Antica to Dolin Rouge)**
- **5 dashes Angostura Bitters**
- **3 dashes Regan's Orange Bitters**

1. Combine all of the ingredients in a mixing glass with ice, stir until chilled and dilluted, and strain into the chilled Nick and Nora glass; strain the remainder of the cocktail into a mini carafe that sits on ice.

2. Garnish with cherries on a skewer.

CAPITOL BAR
1440 NE BROADWAY

Upon first moving to NE Portland, this corner bar became an instant favorite. Their wings are absolutely delicious and their cocktails are top notch. Making friends with the bartender resulted in being provided with this excellent recipe.

· POMEGRANATE COSMO ·

This is one of the most delicious cosmos you will ever have. Pama adds sweetness and punch, while the rest of the drink stays pretty true to the original.

GLASSWARE: Cocktail glass

- 1 ½ oz. vodka
- ½ oz. Pama Pomegranate Liqueur
- ½ oz. dry Curaçao
- ½ oz. fresh lime juice
- ½ oz. pomegranate juice

1. Combine all of the ingredients in a cocktail shaker with ice, shake well, and strain into the cocktail glass.

CEREUS PDX

1465 NE PRESCOTT ST., SUITE F

Cereus was originally conceived as an idea to deconstruct tiki to its most basic foundation and reimagine it through a different lens. The aim is to not only transport guests but to bring cocktails and food from regions of the world that residents of the Pacific Northwest have likely never enjoyed. The entire staff is from Colombia. This new restaurant is surely going to be a smash here in Portland.

Cereus attempts to make their cocktails both exciting and balanced. They have achieved their goal with this one, thanks in great part to the reverse dry shake. With reverse dry shaking, you first shake everything with ice and then strain everything and shake again without ice before serving. Be careful! There is no suction during dry shaking and this can end in a mess. Hold down the shaker top tightly to avoid this.

GLASSWARE: Highball glass

GARNISH: Mint, freshly grated nutmeg, and orange swath

- 1 oz. Wild Turkey Bourbon 81
- ½ oz. Branca Menta
- ½ oz. Grand Marnier
- 1 oz. nitro cold brew
- ¼ oz. rich demerara syrup (2:1)
- 2 dashes 18.21 Japanese Chili Lime Bitters

1. Combine all of the ingredients in a cocktail shaker with ice, shake well, and strain into a mixing glass.

2. Return the cocktail to the shaker without ice, shake well, and pour into the highball glass over ice.

3. Garnish with the mint, freshly grated nutmeg, and orange swath, after expressing the oils over the top of the drink.

· THE PRINCE OF EDINIA ·

This marriage of Latin flavors was created for an event in Mexico and combines tequila with Peruvian chicha morada.

GLASSWARE: Large goblet
GARNISH: Pineapple leaves, dried lime wheel,
and spent pineapple wedge from Chica Morada

- 1½ oz. 100% agave blanco tequila (Cereus uses El Jimador)
- 1 ½ oz. Homemade Chicha Morada*
- ½ oz. Ginger-Cayenne Syrup (equal parts by weight sugar, peeled ginger, and water)
- 1 oz. fresh lime juice
- 1 egg white (or aquafaba for vegan option)

1. Combine all of the ingredients in a cocktail shaker with ice, shake well, and strain into a mixing glass.

2. Return the cocktail to the shaker without ice, shake well, and pour into the goblet.

3. Garnish with the pineapple leaves, dried lime wheel, and spent pineapple wedge.

CHICHA MORADA: In a large pot, combine 5.5 liters water, 15 oz. Peruvian purple corn, and 2 oz. fresh lemon juice and simmer for 1 hour (reducing the volume by about 20%). After 1 hour, add 10 cloves, 6 cinnamon sticks, and 1 whole pineapple and let cook for about 15 more minutes. Remove the pot from heat, strain out the solids, and refrigerate to cool. Add 2 cups sugar and the fruit of half a pineapple, and refrigerate for 24 hours. Strain and enjoy.

EXPATRIATE

5424 NE 30TH AVE.

Expatriate is definitely a unique experience, and that's saying something in Portland. Pairing interesting and traditional "drinking snacks" with classic cocktails, this bar is sure to be memorable.

· SCANDINAVIAN DAIQUIRI ·

This Kyle Webster cocktail is simple but exquisite, much like Expatriate itself.

GLASSWARE: Chilled cocktail glass
GARNISH: Star anise pod

- 2 oz. Aquavit
- 1 oz. fresh lime juice
- ¾ oz. simple syrup

1. Combine all of the ingredients in a cocktail shaker with ice, shake well, and strain into the cocktail glass.

2. Garnish with the star anise pod.

HALE PELE
2733 NE BROADWAY

Hale Pele is amazing—there's no other way to describe it. Nestled between a donut shop and fireplace store on NE Broadway, this tiny little tiki bar is an experience you will not forget. It's fun, delicious, and comes complete with sound effects if someone should order the special drink. Walking into Hale Pele feels like walking into a restaurant at Disney World. It's themetastic!

• SECRET OF THE LOST LAGOON •

Sierra Kirk's prize-winning cocktail from the 2015 TikiTender competition features a combination of enticing flavors.

GLASSWARE: Double old-fashioned glass
GARNISH: Pineapple leaf and edible orchid

- 1½ oz. Coruba Dark Rum
- ½ oz. Wray & Nephew White Overproof Rum
- ¾ oz. fresh lime juice
- ½ oz. pineapple juice
- ½ oz. cold-brew coffee
- ½ oz. ginger syrup
- ¾ oz. vanilla syrup

1. Combine all of the ingredients in a cocktail shaker with crushed ice, shake well, and pour into the double old-fashioned glass.

2. Garnish with the pineapple frond and orchid.

Take a break with this delicious Mindy Kucan cocktail, featuring wine and gin and juice. Yummy.

GLASSWARE: Collins glass

GARNISH: Edible flowers and a mint sprig

- 2 oz. Underwood Rosé
- ½ oz. gin
- 1 oz. fresh lemon juice
- ¾ oz. Grapefruit-Cinnamon Syrup
- 1 oz. sparkling water

1. Combine the rosé, gin, lemon juice, and syrup in a collins glass, fill with crushed ice, top with sparkling water, and stir.

2. Garnish with the edible flowers and mint sprig.

GRAPEFRUIT-CINNAMON SYRUP: Combine 1 part sugar and 1 part water in a saucepan and bring to a boil. Once the sugar is dissolved, add ground cinnamon to taste. Once the mixture cools, add 1 part fresh grapefruit juice. Keep refrigerated for up to 2 weeks.

· SUGAR REPORT ·

Oh man. This Kat Murphy cocktail is amazing. Flavorful and refreshing, you'll definitely want to report for this sugar.

GLASSWARE: Pilsner glass
GARNISH: Cucumber coin dipped
in pink Hawaiian salt and edible orchid

- Cucumber coin
- 1 oz. silver cachaça
- 1 oz. Plantation 3-Star Rum
- ¼ oz. Pierre Ferrand Dry Curaçao
- ¼ oz. fresh lime juice
- ¼ oz. fresh lemon juice
- 1 oz. pineapple juice
- ¼ oz. demerara syrup
- 2 dashes hibiscus water
- ¼ oz. Coco Lopez Cream of Coconut
- Soda

1. Muddle the cucumber coin in the pilsner glass and then add ice cubes to the glass.

2. Combine the rest of the ingredients, except the cream of coconut and soda, in a cocktail shaker without ice and shake well.

3. Add the cream of coconut to the shaker, shake just to mix, and pour into the prepared pilsner glass.

4. Top with soda to create a foamy head and garnish with the cucumber coin dipped in pink Hawaiian salt and orchid.

· SLEEPING LOTUS ·

There is nothing sleepy about this Sierra Kirk cocktail.

GLASSWARE: Collins glass

GARNISH: Mint sprig and edible flower

- 3 mint leaves
- 2 oz. gin
- 1 oz. orgeat
- ¾ oz. fresh lemon juice
- 2 dashes orange bitters

1. Muddle the mint leaves in a cocktail shaker and then add the remaining ingredients with ice, shake well, and double-strain into the collins glass.

2. Add crushed ice to the glass and garnish with the mint sprig and edible flower.

· A'A'PO'E ·

The a'a'po'e (ah-ah-po-eh) are little lava people that keep the mountain from blowing up. This drink created by Paddy Holland is sure to quench your thirst and keep you from blowing up.

GLASSWARE: Super thistle glass
GARNISH: Edible orchid

- 1½ oz. Coruba Dark Rum
- 1 oz. gin
- ¼ oz. grenadine
- 1½ oz. passion fruit syrup
- ¼ oz. Don's Spices (equal

parts Vanilla Syrup and
Allspice Dram)
- 1 oz. fresh lemon juice
- 1 oz. soda to top

1. Combine all of the ingredients, except the soda, in a mixing glass with crushed ice, stir, and pour into the super thistle glass.

2. Add crushed ice, top with soda, and garnish with the orchid.

VANILLA SYRUP: Combine 1 cup water with 1 cup sugar in a small saucepan over medium heat and stir until the sugar dissolves completely. Remove the pan from heat and add 1 vanilla bean, split lengthwise. Let the mixture steep for several hours and then strain it into a jar or bottle. It will keep, tightly sealed and refrigerated, for up to 1 month.

ALLSPICE DRAM: Coarsely grind ¼ cup whole allspice in a spice grinder, or use a mortar and pestle, to achieve large pieces, not a fine grind. Place the allspice in a sealable glass jar and add 1 cup white rum, making sure to cover the allspice. Seal, shake well, and let it steep for 4 days; shake once a day. On day 5, put a cinnamon stick in the jar and shake. After at least a week, and 12 to 14 days total steeping, strain through a fine-mesh sieve. Then strain again through cheesecloth or a coffee filter into a clean glass jar. Combine 1½ cups water and ⅔ cup brown sugar, or demerara sugar, in a small saucepan over medium-high heat and bring to a boil, stirring often. Remove the pan from heat and, once cool, add the syrup to the allspice mixture. Shake and refrigerate for 2 to 4 days before using.

· POLE STAR ·

What the heck is herbsainte? Herbsainte is an anise-flavored liqueur originally created as an absinthe substitute in New Orleans. It is currently produced by the Sazerac company. And a pole star is the same as the North Star—the brightest star that appears nearest to either celestial pole at any particular time. This Paddy Holland cocktail is a pretty bright star too, and that's saying something at Hale Pele.

GLASSWARE: Double old-fashioned glass
GARNISH: Lime wheel and cinnamon stick

- 1 oz. Hamilton Pot-Still Gold
- ¾ oz. Hamilton 151
- 1 barspoon Herbsainte
- 1 oz. fresh lime juice
- ½ oz. cinnamon syrup
- ½ oz. vanilla syrup

1. Combine all of the ingredients in a cocktail shaker with crushed ice, shake well, and pour into the double old-fashioned glass.

2. Top with crushed ice and garnish with the lime wheel and cinnamon stick.

· TICO TICO ·

"Tico" is a term used for natives of Costa Rica. Perhaps this Tara McCarron cocktail is so-named because of its combination of tropical fruits and cachaça, both of which make the drinker feel like they have entered a tropical paradise.

GLASSWARE: Double old-fashioned glass
GARNISH: Pineapple leaf and orange slice

- 2 oz. silver cachaça, such as Avua or Novo Fogo
- ½ oz. Pierre Ferrand Dry Curaçao
- 1 oz. ginger syrup
- 1 oz. fresh lime juice
- ½ oz. pineapple juice

1. Combine all of the ingredients in a cocktail shaker with crushed ice, shake well, and pour into the double old-fashioned glass.

2. Top with crushed ice and garnish with the pineapple leaf and orange slice.

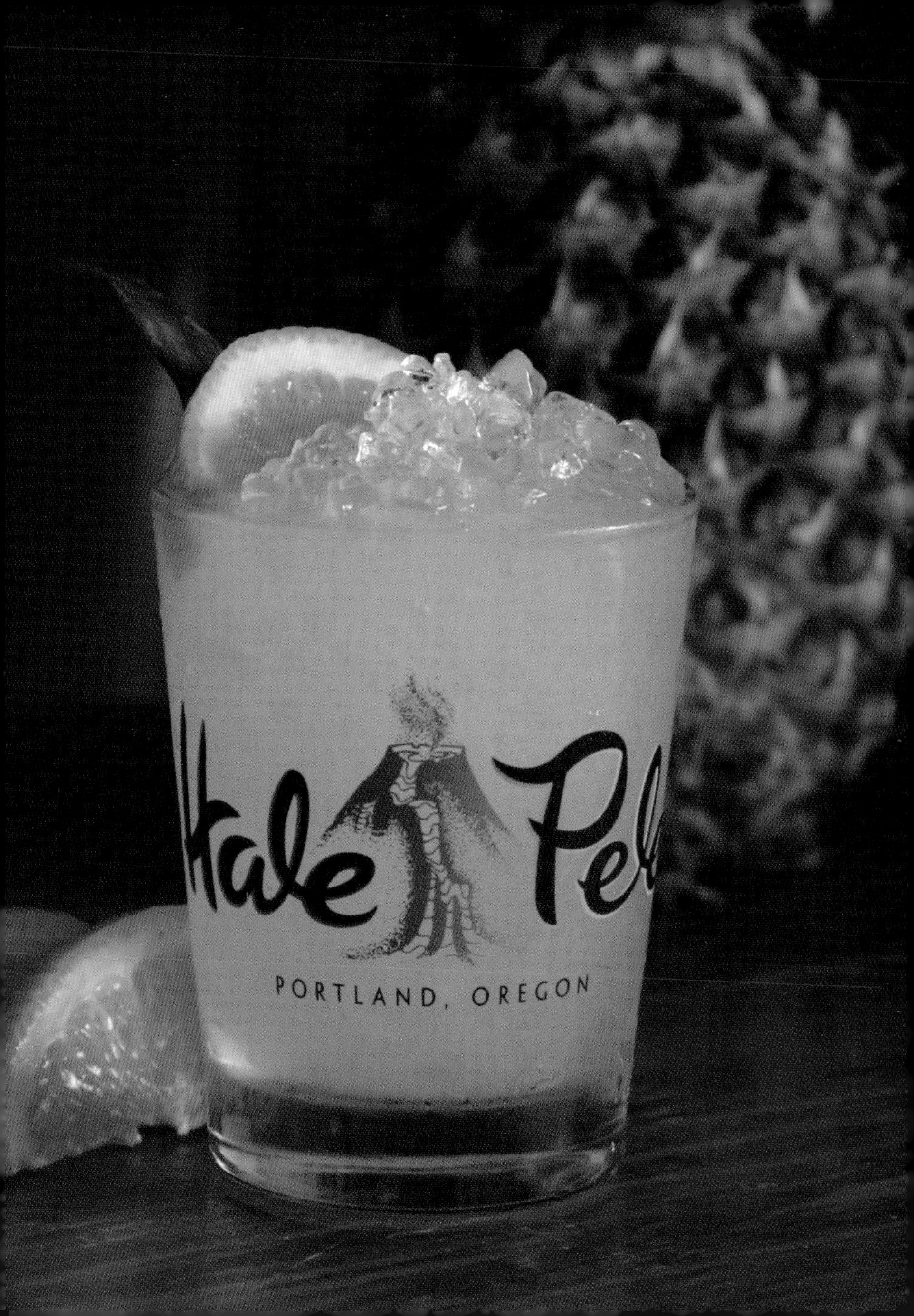
Hale Pele
PORTLAND, OREGON

· SIGNAL FIRE ·

Tara McCarron's combination of citrus, coconut, fruity peach, cinnamon, and overproof rum makes this cocktail a unique delight!

GLASSWARE: Mai tai glass
GARNISH: Two pineapple leaves and lime shell fire

- 1½ oz. Wray & Nephew White Overproof Rum
- ½ oz. Coco Lopez
- ½ oz. peach liqueur
- ¾ oz. fresh lemon juice
- ¼ oz. orange juice
- ½ oz. cinnamon syrup

1. Combine all of the ingredients in a cocktail shaker with ice, shake well, and pour into the mai tai glass.

2. Garnish with two pineapple fronds and lime shell fire.

· HURRICANE DROPS ·

A nother yummy concoction from Kat Murphy. Tropical fruits mixed with ginger, gin, and rum. In a word—delightful.

GLASSWARE: Collins glass

GARNISH: Three pineapple leaves and an edible orchid

- 1 oz. Plantation 3-Star Rum
- ½ oz. gin
- ¾ oz. fresh lemon juice
- 1 oz. pineapple juice
- 1 oz. guava puree
- ¾ oz. ginger syrup
- 1 barspoon Herbsainte
- 4 dashes Angostura Bitters

1. Combine all of the ingredients, except for the bitters, in a mixing glass with 2 oz. crushed ice and stir until foamy. Pour into the collins glass.

2. Add the bitters, top with more crushed ice, and garnish with the pineapple leaves and orchid.

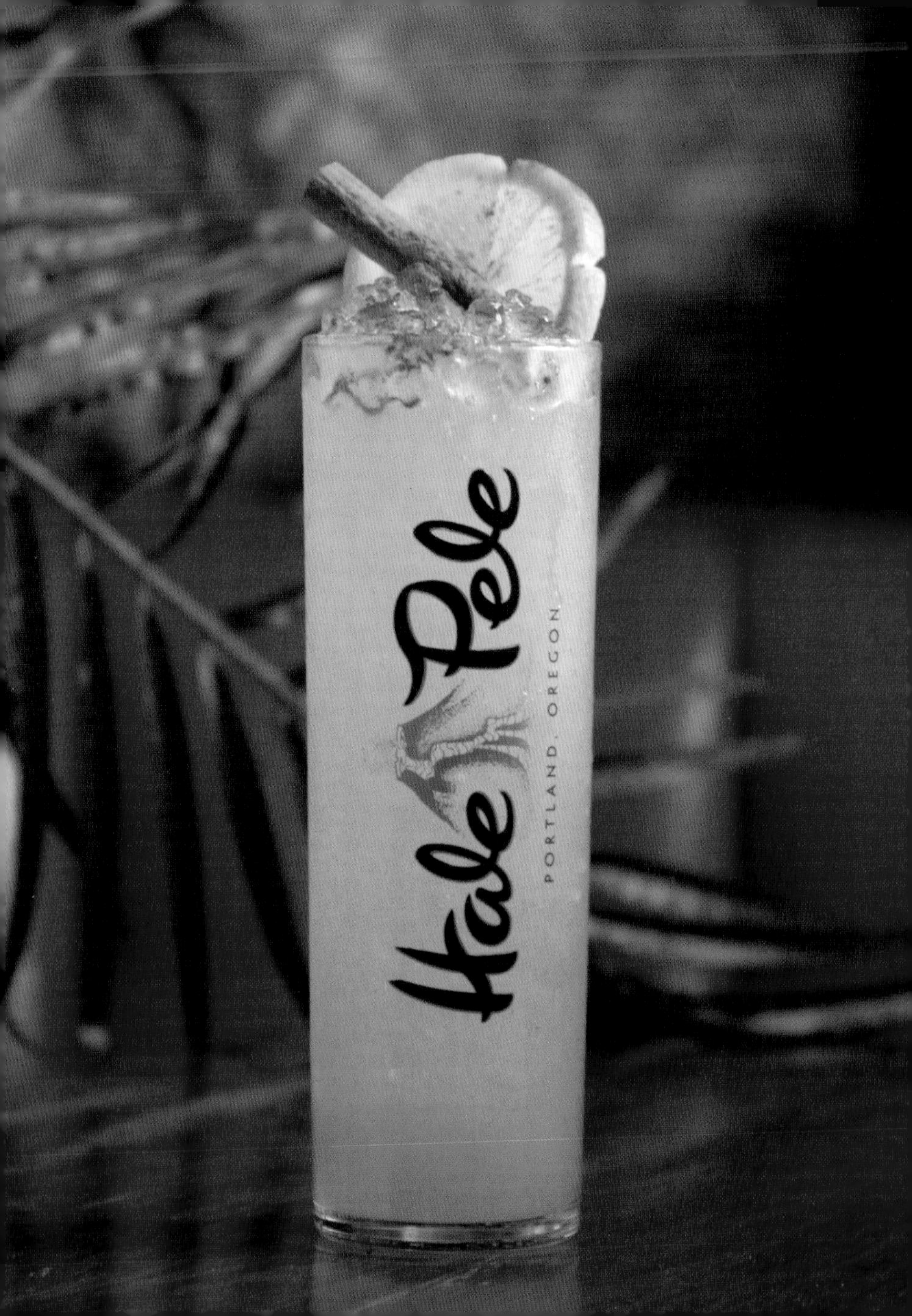
Hale Pele
PORTLAND, OREGON

· THE DUKE ·

t's unclear why this Lindsey Dixon cocktail is called "The Duke," however, it could be because of a famous cocktail called "Duke's Pearl." Either way, this cocktail is sure to reign supreme.

GLASSWARE: Collins glass

GARNISH: Lemon wheel, cinnamon stick, and ground cinnamon

- 2 oz. Hamilton Pot-Still Gold
- ¾ oz. apricot liqueur
- ½ oz. Don's Spices (see page 96)
- ¾ oz. fresh lemon juice
- ½ oz. cinnamon syrup

1. Combine all of the ingredients in a mixing glass with crushed ice, stir well, and pour into the collins glass.

2. Top with more crushed ice and garnish with the lemon wheel and cinnamon stick, and then a dusting of ground cinnamon.

• CHILI CHILLY BANG BANG •

This drink is a perfect mix of flavor and heat.

GLASSWARE: Tiki mug

- Angostura 5-Year Rum
- 2 oz. Angostura Bitters
- 1 oz. ginger syrup
- 1 oz. Coco Lopez Cream of Coconut

- 1½ oz. fresh lime juice
- ¾ oz. pineapple juice
- A handful of mint
- A 2-second squirt of sriracha
- 10 oz. crushed ice

1. Combine all of the ingredients in a blender and puree on high until well blended.

2. Pour into the mug.

OX RESTURANT

2225 NE MARTIN LUTHER
KING JR. BLVD.

· OX BLOOD COCKTAIL ·

Recipe from *Around the Fire* by Greg Denton and Gabrielle Quinonez Denton with Stacy Adimando.

GLASSWARE: Rocks glass

GARNISH: Tarragon sprig

- 1½ oz. bourbon
- 1 oz. Beet Syrup
- ¾ oz. fresh lemon juice
- 1 pinch of kosher salt

1. Combine all of the ingredients in a cocktail shaker with ice, shake well, and double-strain into the rocks glass over ice.

2. Garnish with the tarragon sprig.

BEET SYRUP: In a small, nonreactive saucepan over medium heat, combine 1 cup beet juice and ⅓ cup cane sugar, stirring constantly until the sugar dissolves. Let the syrup cool completely. Refrigerate in a sealed container for up to 1 week (though the syrup is best when used right away).

SW PORTLAND

RED RUM

DEMON'S BITE

GRAVE WATER

MONKEY 'S PAW

HELLFIRE

LAST-MINUTE GIFT

THE BABY DILL

HUBER'S FAMOUS SPANISH COFFEE

A LA LOUISIANE

SW Portland. Home of downtown Portland, with theaters, Pioneer Square, and the West Hills. SW Portland almost feels like classic Portland, a place that changes but also stays the same. Luckily, the changes that do occur are great ones, like the recent addition of Raven's Manor. SW Portland is fun to walk around and explore. You can even catch a show if you're lucky, or a soccer game at Providence Park, the Timbers stadium.

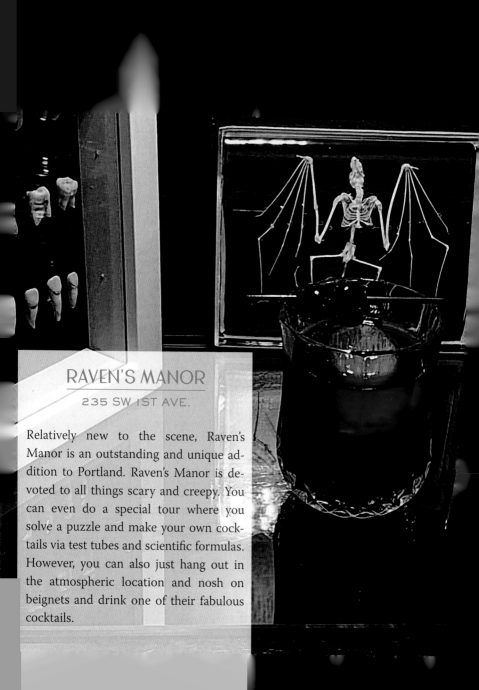

RAVEN'S MANOR
235 SW 1ST AVE.

Relatively new to the scene, Raven's Manor is an outstanding and unique addition to Portland. Raven's Manor is devoted to all things scary and creepy. You can even do a special tour where you solve a puzzle and make your own cocktails via test tubes and scientific formulas. However, you can also just hang out in the atmospheric location and nosh on beignets and drink one of their fabulous cocktails.

· RED RUM ·

"Red Rum, red rum." Who could forget that scene in *The Shining*? Hopefully this drink won't involve murder though, just deliciousness.

GLASSWARE: Cocktail glass

GARNISH: Two Luxardo cherries

- 2 oz. Plantation 5-Year Rum
- 1 oz. sweet vermouth
- ¼ oz. Luxardo Cherry Syrup
- ¼ oz. organic beet juice

1. Combine all of the ingredients in a cocktail shaker with ice, shake well, and strain into the cocktail glass.

2. Garnish with the cherries.

• DEMON'S BITE •

Yes, the name should give you a clue—this drink is spicy!

GLASSWARE: Cocktail glass
GARNISH: Serrano pepper horns

- 2 serrano pepper slices
- 2 cucumber slices
- 4 mint leaves

- 2 oz. Aria Portland Dry Gin
- ¾ oz. fresh lime juice
- ½ oz. simple syrup

1. Heavily muddle the pepper and cucumber slices in a cocktail shaker. Add the mint and muddle it lightly, so as not to create a bitter flavor.

2. Add the remaining ingredients to the cocktail shaker with ice, shake well, and double-strain into the cocktail glass.

3. Garnish with the serrano pepper horns.

· GRAVE WATER ·

Better than the name suggests. Flavorful and botanical, this cocktail is refreshing and interesting.

GLASSWARE: Cocktail glass
GARNISH: Rose petal

- 1 cucumber slice
- 2 oz. Ketel One Vodka
- 1 oz. Ketel One Botanical Grapefruit and Rose Vodka
- 1 oz. St. Germain Elderflower Liqueur
- ½ oz. rose water
- 1 oz. unsweetened grapefruit juice

1. Muddle the cucumber slice in a cocktail shaker.

2. Add the remaining ingredients to the cocktail shaker with ice, shake well, and double-strain into the cocktail glass.

3. Garnish with the rose petal.

• MONKEY'S PAW •

Tropical and a little bit unique, this one's pure Raven's Manor.

GLASSWARE: Coupe, rimmed with 60% dark cocoa powder

GARNISH: Flaming banana

- 1oz. Caribbean black spiced rum
- 1oz. Lillet Blanc
- 1oz. Giffard Premium Banane du Bresil

1. Combine all of the ingredients in a mixing glass with ice, stir for 35 turns, and strain into the prepared coupe.

2. Garnish with the flaming banana.

· HELLFIRE ·

I t's red and it combines cinnamon and bourbon, so you know it's going to be bringing some delicious heat a la a Fireball.

GLASSWARE: Rocks glass

- 1 blood orange moon
- 1 Luxardo cherry
- 1 dash of bitters
- 1 dash of Luxardo cherry syrup

- ¾ oz. Grand Marnier
- 1 dash cinnamon
- 2 oz. bourbon

1. Add the blood orange, cherry, bitters, and syrup to the rocks glass.

2. Add the Grand Marnier to a large snifter, ignite it, and swirl until hot.

3. Pour the flaming stream over the fruits and let them caramelize; add the cinnamon to the fire.

4. Gently muddle the caramelized fruit, not to crush them but to express their oils into the drink.

5. Add a single large ice cube to the glass, top with your bourbon of choice, and stir with a barspoon until chilled.

BACCHUS BAR

422 SW BROADWAY

Located in the Kimpton Hotel Vintage in Downtown Portland,
Bacchus Bar is a fun bar featuring games and live music.

This cocktail is a twist on fruitcake of all things. Nathan Elliott was tired of the overly sweet cocktails that are prevalent during the holidays, so he created his own that is neither too sweet nor too heavy.

GLASSWARE: Double old-fashioned glass
GARNISH: Rosemary sprig and dried fruit

- 1½ oz. blended scotch
- 1 oz. Spiced Oat Milk
- ½ oz. Dry Curaçao
- ¼ oz. Cherry Heering
- ¼ oz. demerara syrup
- 1 dash walnut bitters

1. Combine all of the ingredients in a cocktail shaker with ice, shake briefly, and strain into the double old-fashioned glass over ice.

2. Garnish with the rosemary sprig and dried fruit.

SPICED OAT MILK: In a sealable container, combine 1 quart oat milk with 4 cinnamon sticks, 2 tablespoons allspice berries, and freshly grated nutmeg, to taste. Seal and shake well, then refrigerate the milk mixture for 24 hours. Strain and bottle it for use.

PALM COURT AT THE
BENSON HOTEL

309 SW BROADWAY

Another hotel restaurant, Palm
Court boasts cocktails, fine dining,
and live jazz.

· THE BABY DILL ·

This cocktail is full of freshness, and the herbal notes of gin mix beautifully with the lemon juice and dill.

GLASSWARE: Chilled cocktail glass
GARNISH: Cucumber slice

- 2 slices cucumber
- 1 sprig of dill
- 1¼ oz. 12 Bridges Gin
- ¼ oz. simple syrup
- ¼ oz. fresh lemon juice

1. In a cocktail shaker, muddle the cucumber slices and the dill between two thin layers of ice until completely crushed.

2. Add the remaining ingredients to the shaker with ice, shake well, and strain into the chilled cocktail glass.

3. Garnish with the cucumber slice.

HUBER'S CAFÉ
411 SW 3RD AVE.

· HUBER'S FAMOUS SPANISH COFFEE ·

Huber's Cafe is known all throughout Portland for its flaming Spanish coffee. Alex Perez has served as many as 200 of these flaming drinks a day for 17 years. Perez claims that Huber's probably uses the most Kahlúa of any bar on earth.

GLASSWARE: Rocks glass

- **Fresh lime juice**
- **Granulated sugar**
- **1 oz. 151 rum**
- **1 dash triple sec**

- **1½ oz. Kahlúa**
- **Coffee, to fill the glass**
- **Whipped cream, to top**
- **Ground nutmeg**

1. Dip the rim of the glass in the lime juice and then in the sugar.

2. Add the rum and triple sec to the glass. With a long match, carefully light the liqueurs, swirling the glass to melt the sugar on the rim.

3. Pour in the Kahlúa and then add the coffee.

4. Top with whipped cream, sprinkle with nutmeg, and serve immediately.

DRIFTWOOD ROOM

729 SW 15TH AVE, PORTLAND, OREGON 97205

Portland has a lot of neat bars and restaurants inside hotels, and the Driftwood Room is another one. This 1950s-inspired lounge and cocktail bar is located within the Hotel Deluxe.

· A LA LOUISIANE ·

This cocktail might have come out of New Orleans in the nine-teenth century, but Reid Cooprider's version is more rye-forward and accented by French absinthe.

GLASSWARE: Coupe

GARNISH: Amarena cherry

- 1¾ oz. rye
- ¾ oz. sweet vermouth
- ¼ oz. Benedictine
- 3 dashes absinthe
- 3 dashes Peychaud's Bitters

1. Combine all of the ingredients in a mixing glass with ice, stir, and strain into the chilled coupe.

2. Garnish with the Amarena cherry.

SE PORTLAND

MATT BROWN
RED BEER

THE HAZY JANE

PORTLAND
PERESTROIKA

WHISKEY GINGER

CANADIAN TUXEDO

LANGA GIN & TONIC

UMIDO

LUCE ALLA FINE

RUM CLUB DAIQUIRI

DRESSED TO KILL

PEDRO MARTINEZ
COCKTAIL

DECI'S ROOMMATE

LOVAGE: A BATTLEFIELD

SECRET LIFE OF PLANTS

THE POWER OF ONE

AME SOEUR

VIOLET FIZZ

THE MULATA DAIQUIRI

HIBISCUS TEA COBBLER

CHERVONA WINE

EAST OF EDEN

RING-A-DING-DING

ISLAY DAIQUIRI

BURNT ORANGE SHERRY
COBBLER

QUEEN OF THE DAMNED

POK POK'S RHUBARB
BLUSH COCKTAIL

AVAL POTA HOT TODDY

HOGSHEAD OLD-
FASHIONED

POOR FARM SOUR

POTA PALMER

MONKEY PUNCH

BILLY'S BLOOD AND
SAND

BILLY BOULEVARDIER

CABLE CAR

THREE ROCKS RUM &
GINGER

THREE ROCKS COFFEE

MOROCCAN COFFEE

COSMIC COFFEE

THE DUDE

MORNING NECTAR

PEAR SIDECAR

S E Portland spans from the Willamette River to neighborhoods like Woodstock and Mt. Tabor. SE Portland is fun because each area has a unique feel to it. From SE Hawthorne and Belmont to Eastmoreland, there's never a lack of interesting sights and places to explore.

BUNK BAR
1028 SE WATER AVE.

This former Water Avenue warehouse is now Bunk Bar, providing a very Portland experience complete with a giant mural and pinball machines.

· MATT BROWN RED BEER ·

This drink capitalizes on Portland's love of beer but spices it up with Bloody Mary mix and limes.

GLASSWARE: Pint glass

- 1–2 oz. Demitri's Bloody Mary Mix
- Salt
- 2–4 limes
- 1 can Tecate

1. Prepare a batch of the Bloody Mary mix.

2. Salt the rim of the pint glass and squeeze limes into the glass.

3. Pour the Bloody Mary mix into the prepared glass and fill to the top with Tecate, taking care not to let the beer hit the salt on the rim.

TUSK

2448 E BURNSIDE ST.

Tusk is a Middle Eastern and Mediterranean restaurant with a light and airy atmosphere that is well represented by the cocktails.

· THE HAZY JANE ·

Tony Contreras's riff on a classic Old Maid leans into Tusk's food menu by using yogurt.

GLASSWARE: Cocktail glass

GARNISH: Cucumber ribbons and dried sumac

- 1½ oz. vodka
- 1 oz. orgeat
- ½ oz. fresh lemon juice
- ½ oz. rich simple syrup (2:1)
- ½ oz. whole milk plain yogurt
- 2 cucumber slices

1. Combine all of the ingredients in a cocktail shaker with ice, shake well, and double-strain into the cocktail glass over ice.

2. Garnish with the cucumber ribbons and a sprinkle of dried sumac.

GOLD DUST MERIDIAN

3267 SE HAWTHORNE BLVD.

This hip bar on Hawthorne Boulevard is a great spot for some creative cocktails and elevated bar food.

· PORTLAND PERESTROIKA ·

The literal meaning of perestroika is "reconstruction" and comes from the restructuring of the Soviet political and economic system. It's unclear if Gold Dust Meridian is trying to reconstruct Portland, but this cocktail is sure to reconstruct your taste buds.

GLASSWARE: Coupe
GARNISH: English cucumber wheel

- 1 lime wedge
- 1 dash sugar
- 2 English cucumber wheels
- 2 oz. Lovejoy Vodka
- ½ oz. pear nectar

1. Muddle the lime and sugar with 6 ice cubes in a mixing glass.

2. Add the remaining ingredients, along with more ice, shake well, and pour the drink into the coupe.

3. To garnish, float the cucumber wheel on top and slide straws through it.

PRODUCE ROW CAFÉ

204 SE OAK ST.

Produce Row has been gracing the Portland craft beer scene since 1978 and calls itself the Food and Drink Hub of the Southeast Industrial District.

· WHISKEY GINGER ·

While Produce Row doesn't currently offer this cocktail on their menu, this riff on a Kentucky Mule is sure to please.

GLASSWARE: Tumbler

GARNISH: Orange slice

- 1½ oz. Buffalo Trace Bourbon
- 4 oz. Fentimans Ginger Beer
- 2 splashes Peychaud's Bitters
- 1 pinch grated ginger

1. Fill the tumbler with ice and then add the bourbon, ginger beer, and bitters.

2. Add the ginger and garnish with a slice of orange.

Nostrana means "ours" and this lauded restaurant aims to make everyone feel at home with their simple regional fare and impressive cocktail menu.

· CANADIAN TUXEDO ·

A "Canadian tuxedo" is a denim jacket worn with a pair of jeans. However, this cocktail seems like anything but a "faux pas." Its name is probably more of a reflection of the Pendleton Whisky used in it, as Pendleton is definitely cowboy country!

GLASSWARE: Rocks glass

GARNISH: Flame-toasted coconut flakes

- 1½ oz. Pendleton Whisky
- ½ oz. orgeat
- ¼ oz. toasted rice syrup
- ¾ oz. Coconut oil-washed Alameda Sherry
- ½ oz. fresh lemon juice
- ¼ oz. Solerno Blood Orange Liqueur

1. Combine all of the ingredients in a cocktail shaker with ice, shake well, and strain into the rocks glass over ice.

2. Garnish with the flame-toasted coconut flakes.

L anga refers to the style of this particular gin, which hails from Piedmont, Italy. Nostrana uses a rotation of fresh, seasonal garnishes in addition to lime, thyme, and other spices, so garnish as you deem fit.

GLASSWARE: Wine glass

GARNISH: Sunset geranium flowers,
chamomile, lime, and thyme

- 2 oz. Elena Gin
- 200 ml J. Gasco Indian Tonic

1. Build the drink over ice in the wine glass.

2. Stir to combine and garnish with the seasonal garnishes of your choosing.

· UMIDO ·

"Umido" means "humid" in Italian, which makes sense when you catch a minty, vegetal whiff of the Branca Menta.

GLASSWARE: Collins glass

- 1¾ oz. Bacardi Heritage Rum
- ⅓ oz. Branca Menta
- ½ oz. fresh lime juice
- ½ oz. simple syrup
- Soda water, to top

1. Combine all of the ingredients in a cocktail shaker with ice, shake well, and strain into the collins glass over ice.

2. Top with soda water and stir.

· LUCE ALLA FINE ·

RECIPE BY NATALIA TORAL AND BUNNY SMITH

Natalia Toral and Bunny Smith wanted a bright, fruity cocktail that didn't rely on citrus, and now we have "light at the end."

GLASSWARE: Coupe
GARNISH: Lime wheel

- 1½ oz. vodka
- ¾ oz. blanc vermouth
- ½ oz. Tempus Fugit Creme de Banane Liqueur
- ½ oz. Citric Acid Solution
- 5 dashes orange bitters

1. Combine all of the ingredients in a mixing glass with ice, stir until chilled, and pour into the prepared coupe.

2. Garnish with the lime wheel.

CITRIC ACID SOLUTION (YIELDS 1 QT.): Stir 4 tablespoons citric acid into 27 oz. water until diluted.

RUM CLUB

720 SE SANDY BLVD.

Rum Club is a must if you like rum. Their New Year's Eve celebration is especially fun, featuring delicious Cuban snacks and amazing cocktails.

· RUM CLUB DAIQUIRI ·

A classic, this of course must be served at a club devoted to rum.

GLASSWARE: Chilled coupe

- 2 oz. aged rum
- ¾ oz. fresh lime juice
- ½ oz. rich simple syrup (2:1)
- ¼ oz. maraschino liqueur
- 2 dashes Angostura Bitters
- 6 drops Herbsaint

1. Combine all of the ingredients in a cocktail shaker with ice, shake well, and strain into the chilled coupe.

· DRESSED TO KILL ·

It's not entirely clear where the name of this cocktail comes from, however, it seems that Emily Mistell could have been inspired by the London dry gin as a James Bond reference.

GLASSWARE: Coupe
GARNISH: Orange twist or grapefruit wedge

- 1½ oz. London dry gin
- ½ oz. Appleton Estate Signature Rum
- ¾ oz. fresh lime juice
- ¾ oz. Grapefruit Cordial
- 5 drops Bittermens Elemakule Tiki Cocktail Bitters

1. Combine all of the ingredients in a cocktail shaker with ice, shake well, and strain into the coupe.

2. Garnish with the orange twist.

GRAPEFRUIT CORDIAL: Juice 2 peeled grapefruits, reserving the peels, to yield about 1 cup juice. Put the grapefruit juice, reserved peels, ½ cup fresh lime juice, ½ cup water, 3 cups granulated sugar, and 1 teaspoon citric acid into a high-powered blender and blend at low speed for 20 minutes. Strain through chinois or a fine-mesh strainer.

• PEDRO MARTINEZ COCKTAIL •

Michael Shea describes this as "a rummy spin on the classic gin cocktail," which combines a rich, hearty rum from Guyana with various bitters and some sweetness.

GLASSWARE: Old-fashioned glass

- 1 small strip lime peel
- 2 oz. demerara rum
- 1 oz. Cocchi Vermouth di Torino
- ¼ oz. maraschino liqueur
- 10 drops aromatic bitters
- 3 dashes orange bitters
- 4 drops absinthe
- 2 lemon twists

1. Squeeze the lime peel inside a mixing glass, then drop in the peel.

2. Add the remaining ingredients, except the lemon twists, to the mixing glass with ice, stir to chill, and then strain into the old-fashioned glass over a single large ice cube.

3. Squeeze the lemon twists over the top of the drink to express the oils, then discard.

OK OMENS

1758 SE HAWTHORNE BLVD.

OK Omens describes itself as a "wine focused restaurant," which explains why their cocktails all involve wine of some kind.

· DECI'S ROOMMATE ·

Alex Blair's refreshing blend of wine and lime juice is perfect for a hot summer night.

GLASSWARE: Rocks glass

GARNISH: Mint

- 1 oz. Calvados
- ¾ oz. fresh lime juice
- ½ oz. rich simple syrup (2:1)

- 2 oz. Demi-Sec Sparkling Rosé

1. Combine the Calvados, lime juice, and simple syrup in a cocktail shaker with ice and shake well. Then add the rosé, without shaking, and strain into the rocks glass over ice.

2. Garnish with the mint.

· LOVAGE: A BATTLEFIELD ·

Love is a battlefield, but this drink by Alex Blair is not. It's just harmony in a glass.

GLASSWARE: Collins glass

GARNISH: Lovage

- ¾ oz. Suze
- ¾ oz. Cocchi Americano
- ¾ oz. triple sec
- ¼ oz. fresh lemon juice
- 1 pinch salt
- Tonic, to top

1. Combine all of the ingredients in a collins glass with ice and stir to combine.

2. Garnish with lovage.

HEY LOVE
920 E BURNSIDE ST.

Hey Love, which sits inside the Jupiter Next Hotel, has managed to create a tropical paradise inside, complete with cocktails to match the theme.

Emily Mistell's twist on a classic Mai Tai combines mango and oolong syrup to create a flavorful and elevated version.

GLASSWARE: Tiki glass
GARNISH: Thai basil bundle

- 1½ oz. white rum
- ¾ oz. Mango-Oolong Syrup
- ¾ oz. fresh lime juice
- ¼ oz. orgeat
- ¼ oz. Velvet Falernum
- 10 drops salt solution (1 part salt, 5 parts water)
- 1 dash absinthe

1. Combine all of the ingredients in a cocktail shaker with ice, shake well, and strain into the glass.

2. Top the cocktail with crushed ice and garnish with the Thai basil bundle.

MANGO-OOLONG SYRUP: In a saucepan, heat 12 ounces water to 195°F and then add 4 tablespoons oolong tea leaves and steep for 5 minutes. Strain the tea leaves out of the brewed tea, then return the tea to low heat, adding 30 ounces mango puree, 30 ounces white sugar, 1 (12 oz.) can of mango nectar, and 12 grams citric acid. Stir over heat until the sugar is dissolved and the ingredients are well combined. Keep refrigerated for approximately 1 month.

QUAINTRELLE

2032 SE CLINTON ST.

A *quaintrelle* is a woman who emphasizes a life of passion, expressed through personal style, leisurely pastimes, charm, and a cultivation of life's pleasures. So it seems this restaurant and bar is trying to keep it simple, got it?

· THE POWER OF ONE ·

Although this is an older cocktail from Quaintrelle's menu, Camille Cavan's creation is still luxurious and delicious.

GLASSWARE: Double old-fashioned glass
GARNISH: Shaved fresh ginger (approximately 1 teaspoon)

- 2 oz. aged rum (Cavan uses Appleton Estate Reserve)
- 1 oz. coconut milk
- 1 oz. fresh lime juice
- 1 oz. rich simple syrup (2:1)

1. Combine all of the ingredients in a cocktail shaker with ice, shake well, and strain into the old-fashioned glass over ice.

2. If you have access to crushed ice, add crushed ice over the top of the cocktail and garnish with the shaved fresh ginger.

· AME SOEUR ·

*A*me soeur translates to a "soulmate" or a "soul sister." This cocktail by Camille Cavan does feel like meeting your soulmate—life-changing, in a great way.

GLASSWARE: Cocktail glass
GARNISH: Edible flower (optional)

- 1¼ oz. cold-brew coffee
- 1 oz. Green Chartreuse
- 1 oz. coconut milk
- ¾ oz. simple syrup
- ¾ oz. Amaro Dell'Etna
- Heavy Vanilla Cream, to top

1. Combine all of the ingredients, except the cream, in a cocktail shaker with ice, shake well, and fine strain into the cocktail glass.

2. Top with the cream and, if using, garnish with an edible flower.

HEAVY VANILLA CREAM: In a cocktail shaker, combine 1 cup heavy whipping cream, 1 oz. vanilla bean paste, and ½ cup simple syrup and shake vigorously, until thick. Keep refrigerated for up to 5 days.

CAMILLE CAVAN
Head Bartender at Quaintrelle

How did you get interested in cocktails?

CC: I worked in one of the first craft cocktail spots in Portland years ago, while working part-time in the music industry, and found the cocktails to be inspiring, elevated, and created with thought and care. I hadn't really seen cocktails to be that elevated before. After that bar closed, I moved to another restaurant where I began playing with cocktail creations and was surprised by how easy flavor profiles, vision, and intuition with what would work came to me. Ironically, I pushed back from being a creator of cocktails, almost saying to myself, "I don't want to be great at this," but eventually gave in to this calling. Also, at that time, restaurant and the service industry culture were not something that felt healthy for me.

Who has influenced you in terms of cocktails, any Portland bartenders or mixologists?

CC: I worked underneath Jeffrey Morgenthaler in Eugene, before he moved to Portland, and I was able to get a glimpse into true hospitality. Aaron Zieske, now of Scotch Lodge, first showed me the care that comes with elevated cocktails and I saw how inticate that could be. However, I find myself to be extremely self-taught, pushing through barriers and boundaries.

What do you think is unique about Portland's cocktail scene?

CC: The Portland cocktail scene has always been a pretty tight community, sometimes hard to become a part of but ultimately a mecca for creativity. I feel the primary reason it is so special is the seasonal produce and close connection to farms we have here. The culinary aspects are above and beyond.

Any favorite stories from your time behind the bar?

CC: There's really nothing better than having a guest order a cocktail, watch you make it, and then watch the joy come over them and get genuinely happy, and their time becomes better because of it. Or if a guest goes out of their way to come and tell you that the cocktail you made them was the best cocktail of their life. That type of story beats any other story, like someone famous coming in or a crazy moment with a guest—there's no better feeling.

What's your favorite cocktail to make?

CC: It varies and changes often. People do not realize how often their palate shifts, how they may really enjoy something they haven't in the past, so I love to make cocktails that someone may not think they want but ultimately end up really making an impression, like a rum Old-Fashioned or a tropical rum-based cocktail with coconut milk.

However, my all-time favorite cocktail to make is a pisco sour. I love the heavy citrus elements, the rustic earthiness of the pisco, and I am a sucker for egg white—anything that's frothy is my jam. I do not trust shaken cocktails that do not have any head.

What is essential for novice cocktail makers to have in their home bar?
CC: The makings for a mezcal negroni . . . but with coffee. Coffee bitters, coffee liqueur, cold brew, whatever works for you.

What is your process for creating cocktails?
CC: I have a very different approach than many. I always think of flavors, profiles, and liquors I haven't used or visited in a while then begin putting combination ideas on paper. I could be waiting in line at the grocery store, on a walk, or making dinner and I will stop and make a note on my phone. I then go to work, and put these flavors together, tweak them, and they either may not be exactly what I had envisioned—in which case I stop the process and discard the idea, because rarely do good cocktails happen when they're forced—or they're gems and going on the menu the next day. I work fast and impulsively, oftentimes creating a cocktail the day I put it on the menu. I also never do whole cocktail menu re-vamps, especially as the sole creator of the cocktail program.

Is there an absolute no-no in cocktail making?
CC: Do not shake straight spirits. Adding more ingredients will not fix a cocktail. Cocktail creation is not about you, it's not an ego trip or something that is for your palate. A good creator thinks about the guest; the varieties of different tastes, what will make them happy and feel taken care of. Lastly, do not take things personally.

What makes a cocktail into a craft cocktail?
The type of ingredients chosen; the care taken for those ingredients; correct execution for each cocktail. This includes ice, dilution, and choosing combinations that highlight each ingredient.

If Portland were a cocktail, what cocktail would it be and why?
CC: What service industry people drink and what the average, every-day Joe drinks could not be more different in this town, so, this is a two-part answer: either a shot of Fernet and a bottle of Rainier or a passion fruit margarita.

PALOMAR

959 SE DIVISION ST., #100

Palomar is a fun and trendy Cuban hangout combining amazing food with even more amazing cocktails.

· VIOLET FIZZ ·

F un and tropical, Ricky Gomez's riff on a gin fizz is guaranteed to please!

GLASSWARE: Collins glass

- **2 oz. gin**
- **¾ oz. fresh lemon juice**
- **½ oz. creme de violette (Palomar uses Bitter Truth Violet)**
- **¼ oz. orgeat**
- **¼ oz. rich simple syrup (2:1)**
- **½ oz. fresh egg white**
- **¼ oz. passion fruit syrup**
- **¼ oz. blue curaçao**
- **1 oz. chilled sparkling water, to top**

1. Combine all of the ingredients, except the sparkling water, in a cocktail shaker, and dry shake to combine, then add ice to the shaker and shake again until well chilled.

2. Double strain into the collins glass over 2 ice cubes and top with the chilled sparkling water.

· THE MULATA DAIQUIRI ·

Ricky Gomez's Daiquiri pairs aged rum with the rich mouthfeel of creme de cacao. This drink can also be blended with crushed ice instead of shaken.

GLASSWARE: Chilled cocktail glass

- 1½ oz. aged rum
- ¾ oz. fresh lime juice
- ½ oz. creme de cacao
- ½ oz. rich demerara syrup

1. Combine all of the ingredients in a cocktail shaker with ice, shake well, and strain into the cocktail glass.

BAR CASA VALE

215 SE 9TH AVE., SUITE 109

This Daniel Parker Guidry recipe is a tart, floral masterpiece that almost feels healthy thanks to the tea.

GLASSWARE: Collins glass
GARNISH: Lemon wheel, hibiscus flowers, and Amarena cherry

- 1 teaspoon grenadine
- 1 lemon wheel, sliced in half
- 1 oz. curaçao
- 1 oz. cognac
- 1½ oz. Hibiscus Tea

1. In the collins glass, combine the grenadine and lemon wheel and muddle until the oils from the citrus are released into the syrup. Add the remaining ingredients and then fill the glass with crushed ice.

2. Stir until the cocktail starts to dilute, then add more ice and garnish with the lemon wheel, flowers, and cherry.

HIBISCUS TEA: Pour 4¼ cups boiling water over 3½ oz. dried hibiscus flowers, steep for 10 minutes, strain through cheese cloth, and bottle.

KACHKA

960 SE 11TH AVE.

Kachka means "little duck" in Belarusian/Yiddish and is a favorite
restaurant in Portland. The food is divine, whether it's the selection
of dumplings filled with farmers cheese and other ingredients, or the
caviar. The cocktails are also memorable and add to the experience.

Never had Hunter's Vodka? Israel Morales's recipe is the perfect excuse to make your own!

GLASSWARE: Rocks glass
GARNISH: Orange twist and freshly grated nutmeg

- 1½ oz. Hunter's Vodka
- 1½ oz. dry red wine
- ½ oz. sweet vermouth
- ½ oz. simple syrup

1. Combine all of the ingredients in a cocktail shaker with ice, shake well, and strain into the rocks glass over ice.

2. Squeeze the orange twist over the drink, add it to the glass as a garnish, and then grate nutmeg over the drink.

HUNTER'S VODKA: In a small skillet over medium heat, toast 1½ teaspoons whole allspice berries, 1½ teaspoons juniper berries, ½ teaspoon whole black peppercorns, ½ teaspoon whole coriander seeds, ½ teaspoon whole fenugreek seeds, 1 stick cinnamon, 1 blade of dried star anise, and 1 whole clove, stirring until aromatic, about 2 minutes. Place the spices in a quart-sized jar and add 1 (750 ml) bottle vodka (save the vodka bottle for the finished infusion). Seal the jar and let the mixture steep for 4 days in a dark, cool place. When the infusion is ready, add 1 tablespoon maple syrup to the reserved vodka bottle. Strain the infused vodka into the bottle using a fine-mesh strainer and funnel. Discard the spices. Close the bottle and shake to combine. Freeze for at least 1 hour before serving.

BIBLE CLUB

6716 SE 16TH AVE.

The Bible Club is a very fun cocktail bar modeled after a Prohibition-style speakeasy. They often have music playing in their outdoor area, and during the summer they have refreshing slushies in addition to their usual cocktails. Additionally, they now have a sister speakeasy in Osaka, Japan!

· EAST OF EDEN ·

Megan Kim's creamy, floral, delicately sweet and bright cocktail tastes like an elegant lavender piña colada.

GLASSWARE: Coupe

- 1½ oz. vodka
- ½ oz. coconut rum
- ¼ oz. cream
- ½ oz. egg white

- ½ oz. fresh lemon juice
- ½ oz. simple syrup
- 2 dashes lavender bitters

1. Combine all of the ingredients in a cocktail shaker with ice, shake well, and strain into the coupe.

· RING-A-DING-DING ·

A smoky, spirit-forward cocktail with strong notes of baking spices, in Megan Kim's words, it tastes "smoky and Christmassy."

GLASSWARE: Rocks glass

GARNISH: Dehydrated orange wheel

- 1½ oz. scotch or mezcal
- ½ oz. Cointreau
- ½ oz. Hamilton's Pimento Dram
- ½ oz. Ancho Verde Poblano Chili Liqueur
- ¼ oz. molasses syrup
- 4 dashes Angostura Bitters
- 4 dashes Fee Brothers Aztec Chocolate Bitters

1. Combine all of the ingredients in a mixing glass with ice, stir to combine, and strain into the cocktail glass, either up or over ice.

SCOTCH LODGE
215 SE 9TH AVE., STE. 102

The Scotch Lodge feels like you are
entering a hidden world. At least the
first time you go there. Once you
enter it's a fabulous and welcoming
place with an incredibly extensive bar.

· ISLAY DAIQUIRI ·

Jessica Braasch's take on a Daiquiri uses smoky scotch to add an extra layer and the pineapple rum with coconut tea ties everything together.

GLASSWARE: Chilled rocks glass

GARNISH: Freshly grated nutmeg

- 1 oz. Ardbeg
- 1 oz. Stiggins Fancy Pineapple Rum
- ¾ oz. fresh lime juice
- ½ oz. Coconut Oolong Syrup
- 2 drops Bittermens Tiki Bitters

1. Combine all of the ingredients in a cocktail shaker with ice, shake well, and strain into the rocks glass.

2. Garnish with the freshly grated nutmeg.

COCONUT-OOLONG SYRUP: Steep 10 grams coconut-oolong tea in 1 cup hot water for 8 minutes, then strain. Mix 2 parts demerara sugar to 1 part tea and blend until sugar dissolves. Keep refrigerated for up to 2 weeks.

n this cocktail, Jessica Braasch combines burnt orange juice with whiskey and sherry for an unparalleled experience.

GLASSWARE: Large goblet

GARNISH: Grilled orange slice and edible flowers

- 1½ oz. fino sherry
- 1 oz. Japanese whiskey
- 1 oz. Burnt Orange Juice
- ¼ oz. fresh lemon juice
- ¼ oz. rich demerara syrup (2:1)
- 1 slice of grilled orange hull

1. Add all of the ingredients, plus a slice of the grilled orange hull, to a large goblet filled with crushed ice.

2. Swizzle the mixture briefly, then top with more ice and garnish with another grilled orange slice and the edible flowers.

BURNT ORANGE JUICE: Halve an orange and place the cut side down on a grill over low heat, grilling until the sugars have begun to caramelize and grill marks appear. Juice the orange and save the hulls.

Matt Kesteloot uses lime and hibiscus to brighten this rye whiskey-based cocktail.

GLASSWARE: Collins glass
GARNISH: Mint and a lime wheel

- 1½ oz. rye whiskey
- ½ oz. cognac
- ¾ oz. fresh lime juice
- ½ oz. Hibiscus Cordial
- ¼ oz. Amaro Nonino

1. Combine all of the ingredients in a cocktail shaker with ice, shake well, and strain into the rocks glass over ice.

2. Garnish with the mint and a lime wheel.

HIBISCUS CORDIAL: In a pot, bring 4 cups water to a boil, then turn off the heat and add 1 oz. hibiscus tea and steep for 10 minutes. Add 1 oz. peeled and sliced ginger, 2 cinnamon sticks, 6 allspice berries, 2 whole cloves, the zest of 1 lemon, and 3 cups sugar, and bring the mixture to a low simmer. Cook for 15 minutes, stirring to ensure all the sugar has dissolved. Remove the pot from heat and let it sit overnight, then strain and bottle the cordial for use within 2 weeks.

POK POK

Sadly Pok Pok is no longer with
us, but this fabulous Thai street
food restaurant has left us with a
cocktail recipe.

• POK POK'S RHUBARB BLUSH COCKTAIL •

Pok Pok was known for their fresh and effervescent drinks, and this cocktail doesn't disappoint.

GLASSWARE: Rocks glass

GARNISH: Orange or lemon twist

- 1 oz. London dry gin
- 1 oz. freshly squeezed lime juice
- 1 oz. Aperol
- 1–2 dashes Fee Brothers Rhubarb Bitters

1. Combine all of the ingredients in a cocktail shaker filled halfway with ice, shake well, and pour into the glass.

2. Garnish with either an orange or lemon twist.

MCMENAMIN'S
LOCATIONS THROUGHOUT PORTLAND

McMenamin's is one of the best-known chains (if you can really call it that) in Oregon. With locations all over the state (and Washington), McMenamin's is known for their beer, cider, delicious pub food, and, of course, cocktails. From warm drinks for cold days to refreshing ones for warmer days, McMenamin's has you covered. It is highly recommended to hit McMenamin's Edgefield for a concert, or just to take in the beautiful scenery from the soaking pool.

· AVAL POTA HOT TODDY ·

There's nothing better on a cold, crisp winter evening than a Hot Toddy, and McMenamin's version will warm you up.

GLASSWARE: Coffee glass

GARNISH: Lemon twist

- 1½ oz. Aval Pota (a McMenamin's exclusive spirit; use any apple whiskey)
- 2 teaspoons honey
- ½ oz. fresh lemon juice
- Hot water, to top

1. Directions TK

· HOGSHEAD OLD-FASHIONED ·

This is a classic Old-Fashioned using a McMenamin's whiskey (although any whiskey will suffice).

GLASSWARE: Rocks glass

GARNISH: Orange peel and a cocktail cherry on a pick

- 1½ oz. whiskey
- ¼ oz. rich simple syrup (2:1)
- 3 dashes Angostura Bitters

1. Fill a cocktail shaker three-quarters full with ice, add all of the ingredients, and stir for 30 seconds.

2. Strain into the rocks glass filled three-quarters full with ice.

3. Run the orange peel around the rim of the glass and use it as garnish, along with the cocktail cherry on a pick.

· POOR FARM SOUR ·

Play around with the red wine you use for this recipe for different ways to complement the whiskey.

GLASSWARE: Rocks glass

GARNISH: Half lemon wheel and 2 straws

- 1 oz. whiskey
- 1 oz. fresh lemon juice
- ½ oz. simple syrup
- ¼ oz. red wine

1. Combine all of the ingredients, except the wine, in a cocktail shaker with ice, shake well, pour the cocktail into the glass, and add more ice.

2. Float the wine on top of the drink and garnish with the half lemon wheel and 2 straws.

· POTA PALMER ·

An Arnold Palmer made with apple whiskey—delicious!

GLASSWARE: Collins glass

- 1 oz. of Aval Pota (a McMenamin's exclusive spirit; use any apple whiskey)
- Equal parts iced tea and lemonade

1. Pack the collins glass with ice, add the whiskey, and fill the glass with equal parts iced tea and lemonade.

· MONKEY PUNCH ·

W hat a monkey has to do with this drink is unclear, but it does pack a mighty flavor punch.

GLASSWARE: Collins glass
GARNISH: Lemon wheel

- 1 oz. whiskey
- ½ oz. Pama Pomegranate Liqueur
- 1 oz. fresh lemon juice
- ½ oz. fresh orange juice
- ½ oz. rich simple syrup (1:2)
- 7-UP, to top

1. Combine all of the ingredients, except the 7-UP, in a cocktail shaker with ice, shake well, and pour into the collins glass.

2. Top with the 7-UP and garnish with the lemon wheel.

W hile a Blood & Sand is a classic cocktail, it doesn't usually include whiskey along with the sweet vermouth and Heering Cherry Liqueur, giving this one a McMenamin's twist. One we very much approve.

GLASSWARE: Chilled cocktail glass

GARNISH: Orange slice

- 1 oz. whiskey
- 1 oz. sweet vermouth
- 1 oz. Heering Cherry Liqueur
- 1 oz. fresh orange juice

1. Combine all of the ingredients in a cocktail shaker with ice, shake well, and strain into the chilled cocktail glass.

2. Garnish with the orange slice.

Billy is busy! Here is his version of a Boulevardier.

GLASSWARE: Chilled cocktail glass

GARNISH: Orange twist

- 1 oz. whiskey
- 1 oz. sweet vermouth
- 1 oz. Campari

1. Combine all of the ingredients in a cocktail shaker with ice, stir, and strain into the chilled cocktail glass.

2. Garnish with the orange twist.

A classic sour.

GLASSWARE: Chilled cocktail glass

GARNISH: Sprinkle of cinnamon and nutmeg

- 1 oz. Edgefield Three Rocks
  Spice Rum (or rum of choice)
- ½ oz. triple sec
- ½ oz. simple syrup
- ½ oz. fresh lemon juice

1. Combine all of the ingredients in a cocktail shaker with ice, shake well, and strain into the chilled cocktail glass.

2. Sprinkle with cinnamon and nutmeg.

· THREE ROCKS RUM & GINGER ·

This cocktail reads as a classic Jamaican Mule. Yummy.

GLASSWARE: 10-oz. rocks glass

GARNISH: Lime wedge

- 1 oz. Edgefield Three Rocks Rum (or rum of choice)
- Ginger beer or ginger ale, to top

1. Fill the rocks glass with ice, add the rum, top with ginger beer or ginger ale, and garnish with the lime wedge.

Coffee with rum? A delicious pick-me-up!

GLASSWARE: 8-oz. coffee glass

- 2 sugar cubes
- 1 tablespoon hot coffee, plus more to fill
- 1 oz. Edgefield Three Rocks Rum (or rum of choice)
- Fresh whipped cream, to top

1. Shock the coffee glass with hot water and then pour out the water.

2. Muddle the sugar cubes in the glass with 1 tablespoon hot coffee.

3. Add the rum, fill the flass with more hot coffee, and top with whipped cream.

O h man, if this is what the coffee is like in Morocco, I want to go to there.

- Orange slice, to rim
- Bakers sugar, to rim
- ¼ oz. 151 proof rum
- 1 oz. coffee liqueur
- ¼ oz. Irish cream
- Hot coffee, to fill
- Fresh whipped cream, to top

1. Using the orange slice, wet the rim of the coffee glass and then roll it in bakers sugar.

2. Pour the rum into the glass and use a long lighter to ignite the rum, allowing the sugar rim to caramelize; sprinkle a few dashes of cinnamon and nutmeg and watch the sparks fly.

3. Add the liqueur and Irish cream and fill the glass with the coffee.

4. Top with the whipped cream and garnish with a sprinkle of the cinnamon and nutmeg.

· COSMIC COFFEE ·

McMenamin's has a passport and calls people who get every stamp "Cosmic Tripsters," which explains the name of this cocktail.

GLASSWARE: Irish coffee glass

- ½ oz. hazelnut liqueur
- ½ oz. coffee liqueur
- Hot coffee, to fill
- Fresh whipped cream, to top

1. Add the liqueurs to the glass, fill with coffee, and top with the whipped cream.

· THE DUDE ·

The Dude abides. The Dude always abides. For the full effect, stir with your finger.

GLASSWARE: **Rocks glass**

- 1 oz. coffee liqueur
- ½ oz. vodka
- Half & half, to fill

1. Add ice to the rocks glass and build the drink.

Yes, this drink will wake you up.

GLASSWARE: Chilled cocktail glass
GARNISH: Orange and lemon wheels

- 1 oz. brandy
- ½ oz. St. Germain Elderflower Liqueur
- ½ oz. fresh lemon juice
- ½ oz. rich simple syrup (2:1)
- ¼ oz. pinot noir, to top

1. Combine all of the ingredients, except the wine, in a cocktail shaker with ice, shake well, and strain into the chilled cocktail glass.

2. Top with a float of wine and garnish with the orange and lemon wheels.

· PEAR SIDECAR ·

This one is a personal favorite—a tremendous variation on a traditional Sidecar.

GLASSWARE: Cocktail glass with a sugared rim

GARNISH: Orange and lemon wheels

- 1¼ oz. pear brandy
- 3¾ teaspoons triple sec
- 3¾ teaspoons simple syrup
- 3¾ teaspoons fresh lemon juice
- 3¾ teaspoons fresh orange juice

1. Combine all of the ingredients in a cocktail shaker with ice, shake well, and strain into the prepared cocktail glass.

2. Garnish with orange and lemon wheels.

CIDER & BEER
COCKTAILS

PORTLAND BERRY PUNCH

RAZZBERRY VODKA LEMONADE

RASPBERRY COLLINS COCKTAIL

JEANNEKE

THE UNKNOWN END

COLORADO WHISKEY SOUR

MOLE YETI

No book about Portland cocktails would truly be complete without some cocktail recipes featuring beer and cider. After all, Portland is known for its beer and cider. With that in mind, here are some recipes from various beer and cider companies headquartered in the City of Roses.

PORTLAND CIDER

This fabulous cider company has two taprooms where you can enjoy a nice proper English pint of cider or a flight of ciders. Luckily for us, they also have cocktail recipes that utilize their wide range of delicious ciders.

· PORTLAND BERRY PUNCH ·

This punch is perfect for a hot summer day and incorporates berries, which are plentiful in the Pacific Northwest. Be sure to have some friends over, because this recipe makes a pitcher.

GLASSWARE: Pint glasses

- 2 (19.2 oz.) cans Razzberry Cider
- 2 oz. orange liqueur
- 8 oz. sparkling water
- Juice of ½ lemon
- ½ orange, sliced
- 2 cups frozen berries (blueberries, blackberries, raspberries)
- 1–2 dashes ground cinnamon

1. Combine all of the ingredients in a pitcher or bowl, add ice, stir, and serve.

· RAZZBERRY VODKA LEMONADE ·

The name seems pretty self-explanatory, and you can bet this cocktail will be berry refreshing.

GLASSWARE: Pint glass

GARNISH: Raspberries, if desired

- 2 oz. vodka
- 1 (19.2 oz.) can Razzberry Cider
- Lemonade, to fill

1. Add a few ice cubes to the pint glass and pour in the vodka.

2. Fill the glass three-quarters full with the cider and then fill with lemonade.

3. Stir and, if desired, garnish with raspberries.

SWIFT CIDER

Every year, thousands of Vaux's swifts roost in Portland's old brick chimneys on their annual migration. These birds inspired Swift Cider's natural process, resulting in ciders made from fresh-pressed, locally-grown apples, natural fermentation, and real fruit infusions.

Here is the Swift recipe for creating your own Raspberry Collins Cocktail. If you like hard cider, this cocktail is guaranteed to make you happy.

GLASSWARE: Collins glass

GARNISH: Lemon wheel and mint leaf

- 1½ oz. gin (Aviation Gin recommended)
- 4 oz. Raspberry Collins Cider
- 2 oz. Topo Chico
- ½ oz. fresh lemon juice

1. Add crushed ice to the collins glass, build the drink in the glass, and stir.

2. Garnish with the lemon wheel and mint leaf.

BEER COCKTAILS

RECIPES BY
ERIC BOTTERO AND
DOUGLAS DERRICK

Eric Bottero and Douglas Derrick used to work at Bazi Bierbrasserie, which, alas, is no longer. But these two have plenty of beer-forward cocktail recipes to share.

I t is unclear why this cocktail is named Jeanneke, unless it's for a sculpture in Brussels, Belgium. One thing is for sure, this drink is unique!

GLASSWARE: Rocks glass

GARNISH: Orange zest

- 1½ oz. Monopolowa Vodka
- 1½ oz. Allagash White or other wit-style beer
- ½ oz. fresh lemon juice
- 1 barspoon Honey Coriander Syrup
- ¾ oz. Aperol

1. Combine all of the ingredients in a cocktail shaker with ice, shake well, and strain into the rocks glass over ice.

2. Garnish with orange zest.

HONEY CORIANDER SYRUP: In a dry skillet, lightly toast 30 coriander seeds and 5 cloves; once the spices are aromatic, remove them from heat and set them aside. In a saucepan, heat 1 cup water until it begins to simmer. Remove the saucepan from the heat and add 2 cups honey to the hot water, stirring well to combine. Add the toasted spices to the honey syrup while still hot and steep for 20 minutes. Strain the syrup and store it in a squeeze bottle.

Delirium Nocturnen, which sounds more akin to a spell from Harry Potter than a strong ale. The end is probably not unknown though; it's at the bottom of your glass.

GLASSWARE: Old-fashioned glass
GARNISH: Amarena cherry

- 1½ oz. Old Overholt Rye Whiskey
- ½ oz. Benedictine
- 1½ oz. Delirium Nocturnum or other Belgian strong dark ale
- 5 dashes Peychaud's Bitters

1. Combine all of the ingredients in a cocktail shaker with ice, shake well, and strain into the old-fashioned glass over four 1-inch ice cubes.

2. Garnish with the Amarena cherry.

· COLORADO WHISKEY SOUR ·

Whiskey sours are classic, and this just appears to be a Colorado twist on a classic. Bottoms up!

GLASSWARE: Goblet

- 1 oz. Stranhan's Colorado Whiskey
- ½ oz. Leopold Bros. Rocky Mountain Blackberry Whiskey
- 6 oz. chilled New Belgium La Folie or other Flanders-style red ale

1. Combine the whiskies in a cocktail shaker with ice, shake well, and double-strain into the goblet.

2. Pour in the beer, creating 2 inches of lacing on top.

· MOLE YETI ·

This seems straightforward but also interesting and delicious. A combination of mole (as in the Mexican sauce, not the underground rodent) and Yeti stout, this is sure to get you in the mood for a fiesta.

GLASSWARE: Goblet

- 1 oz. Dagave Extra Agave Spirit, or any quality añejo tequila
- ¾ oz. Leopold Bros. Three Pins Alpine Herbal Liqueur
- ½ teaspoon crushed chipotle powder
- 6 oz. Great Divide Chocolate Oak Aged Yeti Imperial Stout

1. Combine the spirits in a mixing glass with ice, stir to chill, and strain into a clean mixing glass.

2. Add the crushed chipotle powder and stir vigorously to completely incorporate the spirits and spice.

3. Strain into the goblet and pour in the beer, creating 2 inches of lacing on top.

House Spirits Distillery created this beery take on the traditional gin-centric Bee's Knees. It's bubbly, bright, and perfect for the New Year, or any time. Feel free to drink this up or on the rocks.

GLASSWARE: Collins glass

GARNISH: Lemon wedge

- 1½ oz. gin
- 1 oz. fresh lemon juice
- 1 oz. honey syrup
- 3 oz. Troegs DreamWeaver, or another unfiltered, German-style wheat beer

1. Combine all of the ingredients, except the beer, in a cocktail shaker with ice, shake well, and strain into the collins glass.

2. Top with the beer and garnish with the lemon wedge.

FEEL LIKE BEER (OR CIDER)?

Alter Ego Cider: 2025 SE 7th Ave.

The Place: 1212-D Se Powell Blvd.

Cider Bite: 1230 NW Hoyt St.

Schilling Cider House and Gluten Free Kitchen: 930 SE 10th Ave.

Portland Cider House: 3638 SE Hawthorne Blvd.

Swift Cider Taproom: 100 NE Farragut St., Unit 101

Conscious Sedation Beer Garden: 1505 NE Alberta St.

Ecliptic Brewing: 825 N Cook St.

Hopworks Urban Brewery: 2944 SE Powell Blvd.

Cascade Brewing Barrel House: 939 SE Belmont St.

Breakside Brewery: 820 NE Dekum St.

Von Ebert Brewing and Kitchen: 131 NW 13th Ave.

Rogue Eastside Pub: 928 SE 9th Ave.

TheBeerMongers: 1125 SE Division St.

Steeplejack Brewing Company: 2400 NE Broadway

Belmont Station: 4500 SE Stark St.

LOCAL PRODUCERS

SPICED PEAR FIZZ

BLACKBERRY BRAMBLE

THE AVIATION

AVIATION COSMO

SUMMIT SPRITZ

ALASKAN COCKTAILBARNUM (WAS
RIGHT)

HAVE A HEART

NOGRONI MOCKTAIL

BANANA ORANGE CHAI DAIQURI

BERRY CHAI MULE

CHAI AMARETTO PUNCH

CHAI TAI

CHAI-TINI

___

If you want it done right, do it yourself. This could be another of Portland's mottos. In a city with a reputation for "keeping it weird" in the name of self-expression, it should be no surprise that the city is home to producers making spirits and mixers on their own terms. And while the ingredients are sourced locally, the products are in demand all over. That said, you might not be able to find all of these producers' goods on the shelves of your local stores, which is just another reason to come pay us a visit.

FREELAND SPIRITS

GIN AND BOURBON DISTILLERY

Jill Kuehler founded Freeland Spirits to celebrate the women of craft: "From the gals who grow the grain, to those who run the still, we're creating superior spirits that celebrate all the Northwest has to offer. With master distiller Molly Troupe at the helm of the expressions of gin and bourbon, Freeland is one of the few women-owned and run distilleries ever."

This recipe is pure Pacific Northwest and absolutely delicious! The flavors combine to create the perfect drink for a crisp fall day (or really any day for that matter).

GLASSWARE: Collins glass

GARNISH: Pear slices or thyme sprig

- 2 oz. Freeland Gin or Freeland Dry Gin
- 1 ½ oz. pear juice
- ¾ oz. thyme simple syrup
- ¾ oz. fresh lemon juice
- 4–5 dashes Fee Brother's Cardamom Bitters
- 1 small dash vanilla extract (optional)
- Sparkling water, to top

1. Build the drink in the collins glass, add ice, and top with the sparkling water.

2. Garnish with the pear slices or thyme sprig.

You can't have a cocktail book about Portland and not include at least one blackberry cocktail. Blackberries grow like crazy all over Oregon, and this cocktail uses their slightly tart flavor to create a mouthwatering delicacy.

GLASSWARE: Mason jar

GARNISH: Mint leaves and/or blackberries

- 8–10 mint leaves
- 5 blackberries
- 1½ oz. Freeland Gin
- ¾ oz. creme de mure (blackberry liqueur)
- ¾ oz. fresh lemon juice
- ½ oz. simple syrup
- Sparkling water, to top

1. Muddle the mint leaves and blackberries in a cocktail shaker, add the remaining ingredients with ice, shake well, and strain into a mason jar over ice.

2. Top with sparkling water and garnish with the mint leaves and/or blackberries.

AVIATION AMERICAN GIN

When most people hear Aviation Gin, they probably think about Ryan Reynolds, after all, he is the "face" of the company. Those of us who think more about cocktails than about cute actors think more about the Aviation cocktail, of which Aviation Gin is an integral aspect. Whatever Aviation sparks into your mind when you hear it, you'd be remiss not to try this excellent gin brand from Portland. Luckily, you can now buy it online! Or you can visit Portland and go on a distillery tour that ends with an escape room in Ryan Reynolds's office. However, the Aviation cocktail did come first. Aviation Gin is actually named after the cocktail. Just a little tidbit that might come in handy at a trivia night.

· THE AVIATION ·

While Aviation Gin didn't invent this recipe (it's been around since the 1900s), they certainly need to have a recipe for one. Aviation is a unique gin, and this cocktail definitely makes use of its distinct flavors.

GLASSWARE: Coupe

GARNISH: Brandied cherry

- 1 ½ oz. Aviation American Gin
- ½ oz. maraschino liqueur
- ½ oz. fresh lemon juice
- ¼ oz. simple syrup
- 1 teaspoon creme de violette

1. Combine all of the ingredients in a cocktail shaker with ice, shake well, and strain into the coupe over ice.

2. Garnish with the brandied cherry.

A twist on a classic.

GLASSWARE: Martini glass

GARNISH: Lemon peel and maraschino cherry

- 1 ½ oz. Aviation American Gin
- ¾ oz. sweet vermouth
- ¼ oz. maraschino liqueur
- Bitters, to taste

1. Combine all of the ingredients in a mixing glass with ice, stir well, and strain into a martini glass.

2. Top with dashes of bitters and garnish with the lemon peel and maraschino cherry.

NEW DEAL DISTILLERY

New Deal has many different types of liquor; fifteen at last count. They are all about local and DIY, so very on brand with Portland. New Deal also has a bottle shop where you can pick up some more experimental and limited-release items. Either way, this is a must-stop on a Portland distillery tour!

· SUMMIT SPRITZ ·

Presumably this was so named because it includes Cascadia Liqueur. This cocktail is sure to elevate you to new heights.

GLASSWARE: Wine glass

- **1 oz. Cascadia Liqueur**
- **1 oz. Lillet Blanc**
- **6 oz. Aurora Hopes Pomelo and Sage**

1. Fill the wine glass with ice and add the Cascadia Liqueur and Lillet Blanc.

2. Top with Aurora Hopes Pomelo and Sage.

ARIA PORTLAND DRY GIN

Aria Gin makes dry gin, or British gin. Handmade and batch distilled, the ten carefully chosen classic gin botanicals create a flavor profile that has depth and complexity, but above all a perfect sense of balance. All of the botanicals are certified fair-trade (and 98 percent certified organic), and all of the ingredients are sustainably harvested. Being a British gin, Aria would be best in cocktails such as a classic Bee's knees or Clover Club. Thankfully, Aria also had some recipes on their website that make excellent use of the flavors found in their gin.

· ALASKAN COCKTAIL ·

B ased on the classic Alaska cocktail, this drink is a remarkable blend of gin, yellow chartreuse, and orange bitters.

GLASSWARE: Chilled cocktail glass

GARNISH: Lemon peel

- 2½ oz. Aria Portland Dry Gin
- 1 barspoon Yellow Chartreuse
- 1–2 dashes Regan's Orange Bitters

1. Combine all of the ingredients in a mixing glass with ice, stir for 30 seconds, and strain into the chilled cocktail glass.

2. Garnish with the lemon peel.

· BARNUM (WAS RIGHT) ·

About what, it's unclear. Hopefully not the line about a fool being born every minute (or whatever it was).

GLASSWARE: Chilled cocktail glass
GARNISH: Lemon peel

- 1½ oz. Aria Portland Dry Gin
- ¾ oz. Rothman and Winter Orchard Apricot
- ¾ oz. fresh lemon juice
- 2 dashes Angostura Bitters

1. Combine all of the ingredients in a cocktail shaker with ice, shake well, and strain into the chilled cocktail glass.

2. Garnish with the lemon peel.

· HAVE A HEART ·

If you don't like this cocktail, you may not have one. Just sayin'.

GLASSWARE: Chilled cocktail glass
GARNISH: Toschi Amarena Cherry

- 1½ oz. Aria Portland Dry Gin
- ¾ oz. Swedish Punsch
- ¾ oz. fresh lime juice
- ¼ oz. BG Reynolds Real Grenadine

1. Combine all of the ingredients in a cocktail shaker with ice, shake well, and strain into the chilled cocktail glass.

2. Garnish with the lemon peel.

PORTLAND SYRUPS

A LOCAL COCKTAIL SYRUP COMPANY

Although this company was born through trying to create the "Belgian beer of craft soda," it instead turned into a syrup enterprise, and boy are we lucky that it did. These syrups are absolutely delicious in cocktails or mocktails and the flavors are interesting and inventive.

· NOGRONI MOCKTAIL ·

There are such things as sophisticated and tasty nonalcoholic drinks.

GLASSWARE: Lowball glass

GARNISH: Orange twist

- ¾ oz. Portland Syrups Hibiscus-Cardamom Syrup
- 1¼ oz. Wilderton Lustre
- 1 oz. The Pathfinder Hemp & Root
- 1 large square ice cube

1. Combine all of the ingredients in a cocktail shaker with ice, shake well, and strain into the lowball glass over a single large ice cube.

2. Garnish with the orange twist.

OREGON CHAI
COCKTAIL RECIPES

Ah, chai. While it did originate in India, Portland has certainly become associated with this aromatic, spicy tea. We even have our own chai producer. And guess what? You can make cocktails with chai.

· BANANA ORANGE CHAI DAIQURI ·

Oh snap! A daiquiri which combines banana, orange, and chai? What will they think of next?

GLASSWARE: Tiki glass

GARNISH: Mango slice and orange wheel

- 2 oz. rum
- 2 oz. Oregon Chai Original Chai Tea Latte Concentrate
- ¾ oz. fresh lime juice
- 1 oz. banana simple syrup
- 1 oz. orange-mango juice
- 1 cup ice

1. Add all of the ingredients to a blender, along with 1 cup ice, and blend until smooth.

2. Pour the cocktail into the tiki glass and garnish with the mango slice and orange wheel.

· BERRY CHAI MULE ·

Yummmmmy! A riff of a moscow mule with chai and berries.

GLASSWARE: Rocks glass
GARNISH: Lime wheel

- 12 blueberries
- 2 diced strawberries
- 1 teaspoon granulated sugar
- ½ oz. fresh lime juice
- 1¼ oz. Oregon Chai Concentrate
- 1½ oz. vodka
- Ginger beer, to top

1. Add the blueberries, strawberries, sugar, and lime juice to the rocks glass and muddle until the berries are broken down.

2. Add the chai, vodka, and ice and stir to combine.

3. Top with ginger beer and garnish with a lime wheel.

· CHAI AMARETTO PUNCH ·

Just when you think the classics can't be improved upon . . . well, Oregon Chai proves you wrong.

GLASSWARE: Glass mug

- 1 oz. amaretto
- 1 oz. vodka
- 2 oz. Oregon Chai Concentrate
- 1 oz. water

1. Combine all of the ingredients in a cocktail shaker with ice, shake well, and strain into the glass mug over ice.

· CHAI TAI ·

Yep, they even made a martini better by including chai. Will the wonders never cease?

GLASSWARE: Collins glass

GARNISH: Orange slice

- 2 oz. rum
- 2 oz. Oregon Chai Concentrate
- 1 tablespoon fresh lemon juice
- 1 oz. triple sec
- 1 tablespoon grenadine, to top

1. Combine all of the ingredients, except the grenadine, in a cocktail shaker with ice, shake well, and strain into the collins glass.

2. Add the grenadine and garnish with the slice of orange.

• CHAI-TINI •

Yep, they even made a martini better by including chai. Will the wonders never cease?

GLASSWARE: Glass mug

GARNISH: Candy cane or vanilla pod

- 1 oz. Oregon Chai Concentrate
- ¼ oz. DaVinci Gourmet Madagascar Vanilla (or simple syrup)
- 1 oz. Tito's Vodka
- 1 oz. Creme de Cacao
- 2 oz. soda

1. Combine all of the ingredients over ice in the glass mug, stir well, and garnish with the candy cane or vanilla pod.

ABOUT THE AUTHOR

Nicole Schaefer lives in Portland. She is the owner of Missologist, a cocktail subscription box for women and a popular YouTube channel. When she's not filming or creating boxes, she plays video games for her other YouTube channel (HorrorGirl), paints with watercolors, sees (mostly scary) movies, does trivia, and tries to have as much fun as possible with her husband and two cats.

PHOTOGRAPHY CREDITS

Pages 10 and 11 courtesy Library of Congress.

Page 67 courtesy Teardrop Lounge; pages 68, 69, and 70 by Talia Kleinplatz; pages 72 and 124 by Carly Diaz; page 78 by Michael Irikawa; page 80 courtesy Katana Triplett; pages 84 and 87 courtesy Cereus PDX; pages 90, 94, 97, 98, 101, 102, 105, 106, and 108 by Deanna Kavanaugh & Katherine Murphy; pages 116, 119, and 120 by Jared Bradley; pages 144 and 147 courtesy Nostrana; pages 150, 153, and 154 by Jesse Champlin; page 160 by Emily Bolles; pages 156, 162, 165, and 166 by Aubrie LeGault; page 170 by Jordan Hughes; page 174 by Alan Weiner; pages 178 and 181 courtesy Bible Club; pages 182, 185, and 186 by Jordan Chesbrough.

All other images used under official license from Shutterstock.com.

INDEX

Beet Syrup
  Ox Blood Cocktail, 111
  recipe, 111
bell pepper juice
  Pepper Smash #2, 54
Belmont Station, 233
Benedictine
  A la Louisiane, 131
  The Unknown End, 226
berries
  Berry Chai Mule, 258
  Blackberry Bramble, 240
  Portland Berry Punch,
    219
Bible Club, 12, 178
bicycles, 19
Billy Boulevardier, 199
Billy's Blood and Sand,
    197
Black Garlic Bitters
  The Floating Word, 68
Blackberry Bramble, 240
Blank Slate, 78
blood orange liqueur
  Canadian Tuxedo, 145
Bollywood Theater, 26
Bottero, Eric, 224
bourbon
  Amaretto Sour, 51
  American Troubadour,
    85
  Hellfire, 123
  Mandarin Kiss, 41
  Manhattan and a 1/2, 81
  Ox Blood Cocktail, 111
  Whiskey Ginger, 143
Bourne, Jonathan, 11
Branca Menta
  American Troubadour,
    85
  Umido, 148
brandy
  Heaven, 40
  Morning Nectar, 210

Pear Sidecar, 213
Brazen Bean, 33
Breakside Brewery, 233
Brennan, Lucy, 32–36, 43
brewpubs, 21
Bunk Bar, 136
Bunyan, Paul, 22
Burnt Orange Juice
  Burnt Orange Sherry
    Cobbler, 184
  recipe, 184
Burnt Sugar Simple Syrup
  Department of Agricole
    Cocktail, 79
  recipe, 79

Cable Car, 200
cachaça
  Sugar Report, 93
  Tico Tico, 100
Calvados
  Deci's Roommate, 157
Campari
  Billy Boulevardier, 199
  Canadian Tuxedo, 145
cantaloupe puree
  Melones Con Aji, 65
Capitol Bar, 82
Carey, Bruce, 32, 33
Cascade Brewing Barrel
    House, 233
Cascadia Liqueur
  Summit Spritz, 247
Cavan, Camille, 166–169
Cereus PDX, 84
chai
  about, 256
  Berry Chai Mule, 258
  Chai Amaretto Punch,
    259
  Chai Tai, 260
  Chai-tini, 261
Chartreuse
  Alaskan Cocktail, 249

cherry, Luxardo
  Hellfire, 123
cherry blossoms, 23
Cherry Liqueur, Heering
  Billy's Blood and Sand,
    197
  Last-Minute Gift, 125
Chervona Wine, 177
Chicha Morada
  The Prince of Edinia, 86
  recipe, 87
Chili Chilly Bang Bang,
    108
cider
  Portland Berry Punch,
    219
  Raspberry Collins
    Cocktail, 223
  Razzberry Vodka
    Lemonade, 220
Cider Bite, 233
cinnamon syrup
  The Duke, 107
  Pole Star, 99
  Signal Fire, 103
Citric Acid Solution
  Luce alla Fine, 149
  recipe, 149
Clyde Commons, 42
Clyde Commons' Tequila-
    Sherry Egg Nog, 48
Cocchi Americano
  Lovage: A Battlefield,
    158
Cocchi Vermouth di
    Torino
  Pedro Martinez
    Cocktail, 155
Coco Lopez
  Signal Fire, 103
coconut milk
  American Troubadour,
    164
  The Power of One, 163

—ABOUT CIDER MILL PRESS BOOK PUBLISHERS—

Good ideas ripen with time. From seed to harvest, Cider Mill Press brings fine reading, information, and entertainment together between the covers of its creatively crafted books. Our Cider Mill bears fruit twice a year, publishing a new crop of titles each spring and fall.

"Where Good Books Are Ready for Press"

Visit us online at
cidermillpress.com

or write to us at
501 Nelson Place
Nashville, TN 37214

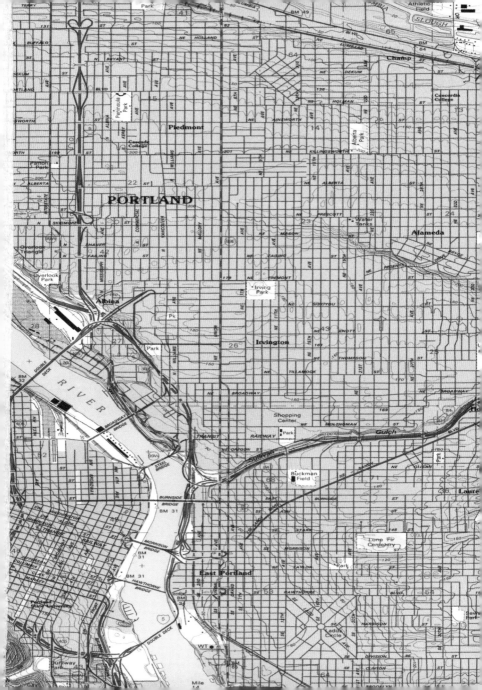